More Ma Library Lessons

Lynne Farrell Stover

Fort Atkinson, Wisconsin

To my aunt Ann, who is also a librarian.

Published by UpstartBooks
W5527 Highway 106
P.O. Box 800
Fort Atkinson, Wisconsin 53538-0800
1-800-448-4887

© Lynne Farrell Stover, 2004
Cover design: Debra Neu Sletten

Contents

Introduction

The popularity of fantasy books among upper elementary and middle school students has never been greater. Students are getting "hooked on Harry" and are more than willing to read other books that have the same themes, similar characters, strange settings and magical circumstances. They are rediscovering such classics as *Rabbit Hill, The Phantom Tollbooth* and *The Lion, the Witch and the Wardrobe* as well as seeking out the newer series, including Lemony Snicket's Series of Unfortunate Events and Piers Anthony's Xanth books.

In an effort to support classroom teachers and their efforts to comply with the current emphasis on specific educational standards, librarians and reading teachers should take advantage of the students' interest in fantasy books. Reinforcing such concepts as fact and opinion, idioms and homonyms will help students with the language section of most standardized tests. While modern technology is quickly redefining the methods in which we search for answers, it is still necessary for students to be aware of the traditional reference materials that are available. Exposing students to the tools and methods of research will prepare them for the tasks awaiting them in higher education as well as the questions they may encounter on standardized tests.

The fantasy books featured at the beginning of these lessons are diverse. They are as old as L. Frank Baum's turn-of-the-century *The Wonderful Wizard of Oz* and as current as Lemony Snicket's *The Unauthorized Autobiography*. There are titles by Mary Pope Osborne for the struggling readers and J. K. Rowling's massive books for the literature lovers. The silly *Matilda* by Roald Dahl can be as enlightening as award-winning books such as L'Engle's *A Wrinkle in Time* and O'Brien's *Mrs. Frisby and the Rats of NIMH*. There is something here for everyone.

How To Use This Book

Considerations Concerning Teaching the Lessons

The 15 lessons in this book were developed for instruction in a library setting during an upper elementary and middle school language arts block. Appropriate for students in grades 4–8, these lessons can be adapted for younger or older students. The lessons need not be taught in sequence, as each one stands alone. With a few exceptions, when it might be necessary for a teacher to continue the activity in the classroom, the lessons can be taught in a 30–45 minute time frame.

Each lesson begins with a quote. These were added to provide a connection between the lesson and the literature and are for the teacher's edification. They may be shared with the students to set the tone, but they have not been incorporated within the lesson itself.

The lessons include visuals and activity sheets. The visuals are designated with an eye icon 👁 and are designed so that they may be made into transparencies and used with an overhead projector. However, you can also copy the information on a chalkboard or on chart paper. The activity sheets are designated with a pencil icon ✏. They serve several purposes. If the activity is a student worksheet it will be necessary to run off the copies needed prior to class time. If it is a game, preparation time prior to the lesson will also be required.

Each lesson contains an evaluation and an extension. The evaluation is usually subjective. The purpose is to give the teacher an idea how well the students have mastered the concept taught. The extension could also be considered enrichment. Whereas the lessons can be taught to an entire class, the extensions are usually for a smaller group of students who have the time and desire to go beyond the regular lesson.

Of note is the fact that not every student has read (or is allowed to read) the fantasy book associated with each lesson. This was considered when the lessons were written and it is not necessary to have read the books to successfully complete the activities. There are also built-in "loopholes" for students who feel uncomfortable with the monsters and magic that are such a big part of these books.

Sorting Hat Word Sorts

"There's nothing hidden in your head
The Sorting Hat can't see,
So try me on and I will tell you
Where you ought to be."
The Sorting Hat *Harry Potter and the Sorcerer's Stone*

Harry Potter and the Sorcerer's Stone

by J. K. Rowling

Story Synopsis

Upon discovering he is a wizard, young orphan Harry Potter defies his uncle's wishes and enrolls in Hogwarts School of Witchcraft and Wizardry. At school he befriends Ron Weasley and Hermione Granger, attends fascinating classes, encounters bizarre creatures and discovers someone is trying to steal a powerful stone that could bring the wicked Lord Voldemort back to power. Harry and his friends foil this attempt. Because of their bravery, intelligence and loyalty they win special awards and are rewarded the yearly house cup for Gryffindor House.

Introduction

A first year student spends his or her first evening at Hogwarts entering one of the four houses, learning the rules and enjoying a grand feast. Students are not assigned beforehand because the job needs to be done by the magical "sorting hat." This hat, over 1,000 years old, is very wise. When placed on a young person's head, it shouts out the name of the house where the student will spend the next seven years.

Time Required 30 minutes

Objectives

- The students will group vocabulary words in specific categories.

- The students will use varied resource tools to help define words.

- The students will be able to state the reasons words were sorted into a particular category.

- The students will engage in critical thinking as unique vocabulary words are defined and sorted into specific categories.

Materials

- dictionaries, encyclopedias, almanacs and other resource materials

- visual from page 12

- activity from page 13 (Photocopy on colored card stock if possible. Cut out the words and place each set in an envelope. One set will be needed for each student or group.)

- activity from page 14 (Choose Creative Categories **or** Basic Categories depending on the "wizard-friendliness" of the students. Make one copy for each student or group. These categories can also be written on a chalkboard or transparency.)

- scissors

- envelopes

Procedure

1. Introduce the lesson by explaining that the activity is a word sort. You may elaborate by telling the students that the Sorting Hat at Hogwarts places unknown students in one of four houses and they will be placing unknown words into one of four categories.

2. Display the visual from page 12. Read the two groups and the five words that are to be sorted. (This is an example of a closed word sort, which means the categories are supplied for the students.) If students do not know the meaning of the words, suggest that they look up the definitions in the available resource materials.

3. Solicit student help to sort the five words into the appropriate boxes. Use a water-soluble pen to record the student's responses. Protagonist and champion are examples of heroes; malicious and scoundrel fit best in the villain group. Defeater may be placed in either group depending on interpretation.

4. Distribute the envelopes containing the 30 words to be sorted.

5. Display or distribute the four categories from page 14 into which the words will be sorted.

6. Allow the students 10–15 minutes to define the words and place the words in the chosen groups.

7. Discuss the word sorts as a group. There are no "right" or "wrong" answers. However, the student must be able to defend his or her choice. (For example: Fungi may be an Interesting Edible or found in the Potions Class.)

8. Conclude the lesson by asking the students what they learned. (Possible, and preferred, answers: *Words could have several meanings, dictionaries are useful tools, it can be fun to manipulate words, etc.*)

Evaluation

The following word list contains simple definitions that will help when discussing the logical sorting of the cards.

- alchemist—a person who attempts to make gold

- apothecary—a person who prepares medicine

- barrier—fence or blockade

- cauldron—(caldron) a large pot or kettle

- chamber—cavity, cavern

- charm—enchant, mesmerize or hypnotize

- corridor—passage or hallway

- crumpet—a battercake baked on a griddle

- dungeon—prison or cell

- emporium—a store carrying diverse merchandise

- enchant—put under a spell

- expel—drive out or banish

- fungi—mold, mildew or mushroom

- gallery—covered passage or arcade

- jinx—curse or evil eye

- petrify—turn to stone, fossilize

- potion—concoction, liquid remedy

- ravine—narrow valley, abyss

- smelt—small oily fish used as food

- specimen—sample, facsimile

- stun—knock out, daze

- swagger—strut, parade

- tart—small pie, pastry

- transfigure—transform, change

- treacle—molasses

- trifle—dessert, sponge cake with jam and whipped cream

- tripe—part of a cow's stomach prepared as food

- vanish—disappear

- vault—crypt, chamber

- wing—building annex, extension

Extension

Using the vocabulary words below, have the students participate in an open word sort. In this activity the students are to study the words and note the commonalities between them. Then they should create three to five categories into which the words can be grouped. To encourage creativity, ask the students to think of ways to sort the words so that stalactite and stalagmite would not appear together. (For example: only stalagmite would appear in the group "Words that Contain the Letter 'G'.")

tapestry	restricted	abnormal	tinge
gargoyle	stalactite	smirk	stalagmite
turban	sallow	abysmal	drafts
centaur	transfiguration	quill	galoshes
babble	berserk	yew	herbs

Sorting Hat Word Sort

In which group would you place each of these words?

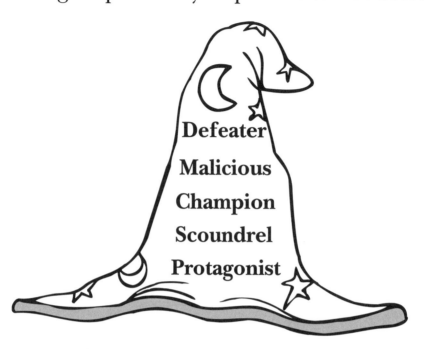

Defeater

Malicious

Champion

Scoundrel

Protagonist

Hero	Villain

If the meaning of the word is unknown, what resources can be used to help?

_____

_____

Can any of the words above be sorted into either category?

_____

Sorting Hat Word Sort
Sorting Words

vanish	cauldron	tripe	transfigure	alchemist
swagger	smelt	ravine	fungi	barrier
dungeon	trifle	wing	tart	stun
vault	corridor	petrify	treacle	apothecary
enchant	charm	potion	emporium	specimen
gallery	expel	crumpet	chamber	jinx

Sorting Hat Word Sort
Creative Categories

Places found in Harry Potter's World	Interesting Edibles
Things Wizards Do	Possible to Find in a Potions Class

Basic Categories

Places	Food
Actions	Tools

Idioms
Six of One,
Half a Dozen of the Other

"In this box are all the words I know. Most of them you will never need, some you will use constantly, but with them you may ask all the questions which have never been answered and answer all the questions that have never been asked. All the great books of the past and all the ones yet to come are made with these words. With them there is no obstacle you cannot overcome. All you must learn to do is use them well and in the right places."
King Azaz *The Phantom Tollbooth*

The Phantom Tollbooth
by Norton Juster

Story Synopsis

Milo, our young hero, is an indifferent student and often bored with his life. One day he discovers a surprise package waiting for him in his apartment. The package turns out to be a magic purple tollbooth. Because he has nothing better to do, he travels though it and enters "The Lands Beyond." He soon acquires two traveling companions, Tock, a watchdog, and Humbug, a talkative insect. The three travelers have many adventures and soon learn the enormous importance of words and numbers. When Milo returns home he discovers that only an hour has passed. He also learns that his trip has taught him much and provided a cure for his boredom.

Introduction

In "The Lands Beyond" there are two ruling cities. There is Dictionopolis, a place where words and letters reign supreme, and Digitopolis, a land where everything is done numerically. It is in Dictionopolis where Milo encounters the members of King Azaz's royal court using idioms in a very literal way. For example, when a "light meal" was served, beams of light appeared on the platters. A "square meal" was one in which tasteless squares were served as the main course.

In this lesson students will work with idioms—phrases or expressions that mean something different from their literal meaning. They will discover that our language is full of many colorful phrases that can be misinterpreted if one is unaware of the connotation of the phrases.

Time Required 25–30 minutes

Objectives

- The students will define the term idiom.
- The students will discuss the use of idioms in the language.
- The students will complete an idiom activity.

Materials

- visual from page 17
- activity from page 18
- pencils and/or pens
- water-soluble marker

Procedure

1. Tell the students that today's lesson will be a literary term that is "as easy as pie" and "a piece of cake," and that they should "get a kick out of it."

2. Display the visual.

3. Read the definition of an idiom to the class and ask them if they remember any idioms that were used at the start of class. Ask the students if they understood that "as easy as pie" and "a piece of cake" meant that the lesson would not be difficult and that "get a kick out of it" meant to enjoy an activity.

4. Ask the students why they think idioms are used in our language. (Possible answers: *Idioms are fun to use. They make a story interesting. They can be wise sayings. They are easy to remember.*)

5. Ask the students if they can think of any drawbacks to using idioms in their speech or writing. (Possible answers: *Some idioms are overused and get boring. Sometimes they are hard to understand, especially for people who use English as a second language.*)

6. Read and discuss the two idioms on the visual. Ask the students if they have any questions.

7. Pass out the activity. Have students work individually or in groups.

8. Allow 10 minutes to complete the activity. Check the answers as a group. (To help the visual learner, make the activity sheet into a transparency and write the answers with a water-soluble marker.)

Evaluation

Answers to the activity:

Six of One: A = 4, B = 6, C = 1, D = 5, E = 2, F = 3

Half a Dozen of the Other: 1 = D, 2 = E, 3 = B, 4 = F, 5 = A, 6 = C

Extension

The idioms we use in our language come from many sources. They may go back as far as ancient Greece or be as current as the newest trend. Some are proverbs, meant to teach, others are slang and still others are just for fun.

Students may wish to create their own idioms. They can use the list below "to break the ice" and get started. They may have some ideas of their own. After all, "necessity is the mother of invention." Who knows? An idiom may be created by a student and others will "jump on the bandwagon" making it part of our language!

What would be a good idiom for the following situations?

1. An adult who acts too much like a child.

2. A problem that can be solved by technology.

3. A problem that was created by technology.

4. Hard to understand television commercials.

5. Clothes that look good but are very uncomfortable to wear.

6. A person who changes their hair color often (or the act of changing hair color often).

Idioms

Six of One, Half a Dozen of the Other

An idiom is a phrase or expression that means something different from the literal meaning.

For example, the idiom "six of one, half a dozen of the other" means things are fairly equal, and there is little choice between options.

In *The Phantom Tollbooth* by Norton Juster, Milo travels to Dictionopolis, a place where words and letters reign supreme. There, idioms are taken literally. This leads to some humorous situations. For example, when Milo orders a "light meal" he is served a platter full of light beams.

"Make Hay While the Sun Shines"

---

* <u>Meaning</u>: Take advantage of an opportunity; do a deed when the time is right.

* <u>Literal Translation</u>: Farmers need to cut the grass in the fields when it is mature and it must dry before it rains.

"On Top of the World"

---

* <u>Meaning</u>: To feel very happy and joyful.

* <u>Literal Translation</u>: A person can go no higher than the top of the world. This expression is the opposite of "down in the dumps."

Idioms

Six of One, Half a Dozen of the Other

Six of One

Match the idiom to the meaning.

_____ A. To be in a dangerous spot.

_____ B. To be brave.

_____ C. To be greedy.

_____ D. To ignore what is said.

_____ E. To make an excellent agreement.

_____ F. To admit you were wrong.

1. Bite Off More than You Can Chew

2. Drive a Hard Bargain

3. Eat Your Words

4. Hangs by a Thread

5. In One Ear and Out the Other

6. Keep Your Chin Up

Half a Dozen of the Other

Match the meaning to the idiom.

_____ 1. Make a Mountain Out of a Molehill

_____ 2. Mince Words

_____ 3. Out of the Frying Pan and into the Fire

_____ 4. Split Hairs

_____ 5. Upset the Apple Cart

_____ 6. Leave No Stone Unturned

A. To spoil a plan.

B. From bad to worse.

C. To make every effort.

D. To exaggerate a situation.

E. Not to say what you mean.

F. To argue unimportant things.

Extra Credit

Can you think of any other idioms? List them below.

1. _____

2. _____

3. _____

4. _____

5. _____

6. _____

7. _____

8. _____

Using Homonyms
Witch Wood Ewe Wont?

"Hour ruler is King Trent, who has rained for seventeen years.
He transforms people two other creatures."
Excerpt from an essay written by Dor of Xanth *Centaur Aisle*

Centaur Aisle
by Piers Anthony

Story Synopsis

Centaur Aisle is Piers Anthony's fourth book in the Xanth series. In this story, Dor, 16 years old and the future king of Xanth, has been left in charge while the current king is visiting Mundania to set up possible trade agreements. When the king does not return at the scheduled time, Dor sets out to find him. Magic may not be practiced in Mundania, but it is still chock-full of dangers. Therefore a centaur, an ogre, the king's daughter and the diminutive Golem accompany Dor as he sets out to find the missing monarch. **Note:** The reading level of this book may be 6.9 but the main characters are teens and act and talk accordingly.

Introduction

A prolific fantasy writer, Piers Anthony loves to play with words. His books, especially the Xanth series, are crammed full of fun puns. Titles of his books, such as *Crewel Lye, Faun and Games, Heaven Cent* and *Night Mare,* are good examples of how homonyms, words that sound alike but have different meanings and often different spellings, are used by the author.

Time Required 25–30 minutes

Objectives

- The students will define a homonym.

- The students will recognize words that sound the same but have different meanings.

- The students will use dictionaries to help determine the correct word to use in a sentence.

Materials

- visual from page 21

- activity from page 22 (Duplicate worksheets for each student or group.)

- dictionaries

- water-soluble marker

Procedure

1. Display the visual. Read the introduction to the class.

2. Question students about the homonyms for the words listed on the visual. Ask for spelling and meaning and record the responses. Possible answers:
   see—to look, **sea**—a large body of water
   to—towards, **two**—a number, **too**—also

there—near, **their**—ownership, **they're**—they are
here—at this point, **hear**—perceive sound
eye—watch, **I**—myself, **aye**—yes

3. Pass out the activity and have students work individually or in groups. Read instructions to the class and ask for questions. Encourage students to use dictionaries.

4. Check the answers as a group when the students have finished.

Evaluation

Ask the students why it is important that the answers be spelled out. (Because the words sound alike!)

Answers to the activity:

1. rowed
2. knave
3. hoard
4. border
5. Baron
6. moat
7. leak
8. presents
9. pair
10. vile

Extension

Students can have fun writing and performing jokes they have created using the misunderstanding that sometimes occurs when homonyms are used. For example:

Diner: *Waiter, I am appalled … there is a hair in my food.*

Waiter: *Why of course there is a hare in your food, sir. You ordered rabbit stew.*

Homonym Word List

- acts—behavior; axe—tool
- ail—sick; ale—beverage
- ant—insect; aunt—relative
- ate—consumed food; eight—number
- beat—to hit; beet—red vegetable
- bite—to grasp with teeth; byte—computing unit
- crewel—yarn; cruel—mean
- crews—sailors; cruise—sea voyage
- days—24-hour units of time; daze—to confuse
- dear—precious; deer—animal
- dual—two; duel—fight
- dye—to color; die—pass away
- earn—deserve; urn—vase
- flee—run away; flea—insect
- flour—grain; flower—a blossom
- great—big; grate—iron frame
- hair—locks; hare—rabbit
- him—man; hymn—song
- in—inside; inn—hotel
- jam—jelly; jamb—side of door
- knew—understood; new—young; gnu—animal
- knight—defender; night—after sunset
- lie—untruth; lye—alkaline solution
- made—prepared; maid—housekeeper
- navel—bellybutton; naval—seafaring
- one—single; won—succeeded
- pear—fruit; pair—two; pare—to peel
- peek—to look; peak—the top; pique—excite, arouse
- piece—a portion; peace—tranquility
- profit—gain; prophet—forecaster
- quarts—units of liquid measure; quartz—crystal rock
- rain—participation; reign—govern; rein—harness
- rap—to smack; wrap—to cover
- rung—sounded; wrung—twisted
- sail—ship canvas; sale—reduced prices
- scent—aroma; sent—launched; cent—coin
- some—part; sum—total
- tale—story; tail—end
- thrown—hurled; throne—king's chair
- use—utilize; ewes—female sheep; yews—trees
- vane—wind direction device; vein—blood vessel; vain—conceited
- whole—all; hole—opening
- week—seven days; weak—fragile

Using Homonyms
Witch Wood Ewe Wont?

What does the above title mean? If you heard it before you saw it, you would have understood it as:

Which would you want?

"Witch" and "which" are **homonyms**, words that sound the same but mean different things and are often spelled differently.

Can you think of homonyms for the following words?

SEE:

TO:

THERE:

HERE:

EYE:

Using Homonyms
Witch Wood Ewe Wont?

Using a dictionary for help, select the word that best fits the sentence and write it in the blank.

1. Frodo and Sam _____ their small boat toward the Land of Shadow.
   road, rode, rowed

2. King Arthur would have to punish the insolent _____ for his bad manners.
   knave, nave

3. To survive the constant winter of Narnia it was necessary to _____food.
   hoard, horde

4. The _____ of the property was now secure and Artemis could relax.
   boarder, border

5. "I know you, you're the Bloody _____," said Ron with a smile.
   Barren, Baron

6. The _____ that surrounded the castle contained more than simple water.
   moat, mote

7. A _____ in the roof of the tree house got Jack's book all wet.
   leak, leek

8. Mrs. Weasley sent Harry and Ron _____ for Christmas.
   presents, presence

9. Crabbe and Goyle were a _____ of boys who were always in trouble.
   pare, pair, pear

10. Mariel of Redwall knew the _____ Gabool would throw her overboard.
    vial, viol, vile

Audacious Alliteration

"I love researching information. It's one reason I love being a writer so much. I especially love visiting libraries and hunting down books that I need for research. It's like looking for treasure."

Mary Pope Osborne, author of the Magic Tree House series

Mummies in the Morning

by Mary Pope Osborne

Story Synopsis

Magic Tree House siblings Jack and Annie travel to ancient Egypt. By using a book as a portal into the past, they are able to investigate a pyramid, decode hieroglyphics and help the ghost of Queen Hutepi find a missing scroll.

Introduction

Most of the books in Mary Pope Osborne's Magic Tree House series and Lemony Snicket's Series of Unfortunate Events have alliterative titles. The technique of creating catchy titles by using repetitive initial consonant sounds has worked well for these authors, as their books are easily identified by their fans.

Time Required 25–35 minutes

Objectives

- The students will define the literary term alliteration.

- The students will be introduced to various alliterative book titles.

- The students will engage in a writing activity creating fictitious book titles.

Materials

- visuals from pages 25–26

- pencils or pens

- index cards or paper

- dictionaries, rhyming dictionaries and thesauri

- several of the books mentioned on page 25 for display, if available

Procedure

1. Explain to the students that when an author writes a book he or she wants to give it a title that is interesting, explanatory and memorable. An author uses words in a title that sound good together. Sometimes alliteration is used to accomplish this.

2. Define alliteration as the repetition of beginning consonant sounds.

3. Display the visual from page 25. Read it to the class.

4. Discuss any other books or names that students know that begin with the same consonant sound. (It is the **sound** that is the defining factor in alliteration. Therefore the author, Carolyn Keene, qualifies as an example. This might be confusing to some students.)

5. Give each student or group a writing tool and index cards or a piece of paper.

6. Display the visual from page 26.

7. Read the directions to the class. Direct the students to the available dictionaries, rhyming dictionaries and thesauri. Encourage the students to use these tools in their search for interesting words.

8. Allow the students 10–15 minutes to create their alliterative titles. (Base the amount of titles required on the ability of your students and the time allotted for the lesson.)

9. Conduct a sharing session by allowing the students to reveal their favorite alliterative title and author with the class.

Evaluation

The following point system can turn this activity into a competition. Students can score another student's or team's work.

- 2 points for each title

- 2 points for each author

- 1 bonus point for each author with an alliterative middle name

- 1 extra point for every word over three words in a title

For example:

The Quirky(1) Queen(2) Questions(3)
the Quality(4) of the Quidditch(5) Quiz(6).

This title would earn 3 extra points.

Extension

Once the students have created the alliterative titles and authors, encourage them to continue the creative process. Have them design a book jacket using their favorite title. They might write a book review for the imaginary book. A list of other books by the same author could be created.

Note: The following Web site is an excellent resource if you wish to develop more activities involving Mary Pope Osborne's Magic Tree House series.

- www.randomhouse.com/kids/magictree house/

Audacious Alliteration

Alliteration: the repeating of beginning consonant sounds.

⁓ Alliterative Book Titles ⁓

Mary Pope Osborne's Magic Tree House series

Buffalo Before Breakfast

Lions at Lunchtime

Midnight on the Moon

Mummies in the Morning

Thanksgiving on Thursday

Lemony Snicket's Series of Unfortunate Events

The Austere Academy

The Bad Beginning

The Hostile Hospital

The Miserable Mill

The Vile Village

⁓ Alliterative Author Names ⁓

Betsy Byars

Christopher Curtis

Louis L'Amour

Theodore Taylor

Vivian Vande Velde

Audacious Alliteration
An Amusing Activity

Using the words listed, create interesting titles for a book you would like to see on the library shelves. Also, using the same letter, make up an alliterative name for the author of this pretend book. Remember alliteration is the repetition of beginning consonant sounds.

For example: palace

---

*A **P**retty **P**itiful **P**alace*

by **P**rincess **P**riscilla **P**atterson

~ Word List ~

- alligator
- bat
- cook
- dinosaur
- elf
- firefly
- ghosts
- horseshoe
- interplanetary
- juggler
- kingdom
- lucky
- millionaire

- neighbor
- overrated
- palace
- queen
- radish
- Saturday
- toothache
- unseen
- vampire
- wart
- xylophone
- yellow
- zero

Anachronism Ad-libs

"Why, in my secret laboratory I have ancient Arabian texts, which will allow me to solve the mysteries of magic and alchemy. Soon I shall have great powers and shall transform common metals to gold, foretell the future, fly through the air on magical carpets! Aye, and even Time itself will do my bidding!"

Dr. Gathergoods *Max and Me and the Time Machine*

Max and Me and the Time Machine
by Gery Greer and Bob Ruddick

Story Synopsis

Young adventurous Steve buys a time machine for $2.50 at a garage sale. This marvelous device conveys him and his best friend Max to a castle and a jousting match in the year 1250. Steve is transported into the body of a young knight, Sir Robert, and Max becomes his faithful horse. With the help of Niles the squire, the pretty Lady Elizabeth and an alchemist, Dr. Gathergoods, they are able to defeat and humiliate the evil Sir Bevis. They have many adventures in medieval England before returning to their proper time in the twentieth century.

Introduction

Time travel has been and continues to be a popular theme in science fiction and fantasy books. The classics, *Time Machine* by H. G. Wells and *A Connecticut Yankee in King Arthur's Court* by Mark Twain, are examples of stories using time travel. The former transports the reader into the far future; the latter returns the reader to a distant past. Currently two popular children's authors use time travel as a method of instruction and entertainment. Jon Scieszka uses a magic book to deliver the boys in his popular Time Warp Trio series to other times and places. Mary Pope Osborne also uses a book as the device that transports siblings Jack and Annie to distant times in her Magic Tree House series.

Many of these stories include anachronisms. An anachronism is the literary term for placing something at a time when it didn't exist. (An example of this would be placing an organization called the World Gladiator Foundation in ancient Rome in the book *See You Later, Gladiator* by Jon Scieszka.) Sometimes this is necessary because of the reader's need for a point of reference. Sometimes an author uses an anachronism intentionally to be humorous. Other times it is unintentional and can be distracting.

Time Required 40–45 minutes

Objectives

- The students will be able to define and identify an anachronism.

- The students will discuss time travel as a plot device in literature.

- The students will complete an anachronism activity.

Materials

- visuals from pages 30–31
- activity from page 32
- water-soluble marker
- pencils and/or pens
- *optional*—books from the library collection dealing with time travel

Procedure

1. Define an anachronism as the literary term for placing something at a time when it didn't exist. Explain that sometimes a writer does this on purpose, either to be humorous or to have something make sense to the reader. However, sometimes an anachronism is a mistake because the author did not have enough knowledge about a historical period.

2. Display the visual from page 30. Read the excerpt from *Max and Me and The Time Machine*. Then solicit suggestions from the students for Part I (the more unusual the better). Write one in each blank.

3. Transfer the student-suggested words to the story of the cave man on the visual from page 31. Read the class-created story to the students. Discuss the questions asked at the top of the visual.

4. Pass out the activity. Read the directions to the students. The activity may be done individually or in groups. Allow 15–20 minutes to complete the activity. Students may wish to share their answers with the class.

Evaluation

The anachronism activities are designed so that students may determine their own points. If the class is working in groups these points become the tool of measurement for team competition. If the activity is completed individually, the points are easily converted into a percentile grade. The questions and lists on the activity sheet are very open-ended and answers will vary.

Examples of possible answers to page 32 from a sixth grade class:

Part I

1. *Jackie & Me* by Dan Gutman
2. *Time Cat* by Lloyd Alexander
3. *Stonewords: A Ghost Story* by Pam Conrad
4. *Timeline* by Michael Crichton
5. *Many Waters* by Madeleine L'Engle

Part II

1. Look Different: glasses, braces, clothing, hairstyle, etc.
2. Talk Different: They spoke English then, but it was very different.
3. Healthier: taller, bigger, more teeth
4. Have More Knowledge: able to read and write
5. Be Ignorant: Would not know the culture or customs.

Part III

The student's work is similar to the visual from page 31. (The words they suggest for the blanks are usually more extreme.)

Part IV

1. Possible Answers: Yes—In the future time travel might be possible. Maybe the UFO sightings people report are actually time travelers. No—If people could time travel someone from the future would have visited us already.

2. Possible Answers: Time travel is a good idea because then we would be able to stop bad things from happening. If we traveled back in time we could change the present and that would be very bad.

3. Possible Answers: Many students of this age wish to travel to the not so distant past to see their parents and grandparents when they were younger.

4. Possible Answers: Students often choose titles of movies such as *Back to the Future* and *Time Travelers*. Allow these answers; they have the right idea.

5. Possible Answers: It is exciting to think you have the power to change things or witness a historical event. People like to use their imaginations.

Extension

Time travel works two ways. While many of the books for young people deal with revisiting a past event, there are some that deal with traveling to the future. Students who are interested in this may wish to make predictions about the world and how it will be in ten years. Have them do the activity below.

⸙· The Future ·⸙

Do you have any ideas about what the world will be like in 10 years? Pick at least 5 topics from the list below and make a prediction about them. Put it away in a safe place. In 10 years, it will be interesting to see if your predictions were correct!

agriculture	entertainment	medicine
clothing	environment	space travel
communication	food	sports
economy	government	technology
education	international issues	transportation

Anachronism Ad-libs

An anachronism is the literary term for placing something at a time when it didn't exist.

Example from *Max and Me and the Time Machine* **by Gery Greer and Bob Ruddick:**

> *"I speak, m'lord of first base, second base, third base and forsooth—home plate! Zounds! For a farthing I would leave my heart in San Francisco."*
>
> —Steve, in the guise of Sir Robert, speaking to the Earl of Hampshire in thirteenth-century England. This is a time long before the existence of baseball and California.

Class Activity — Part 1

Fill in each blank with an appropriate matching word.

1. Book Character: _____

2. Tool: _____

3. Descriptive Word: _____

4. Place: _____

5. Place: _____

6. Action Word: _____

7. Thing: _____

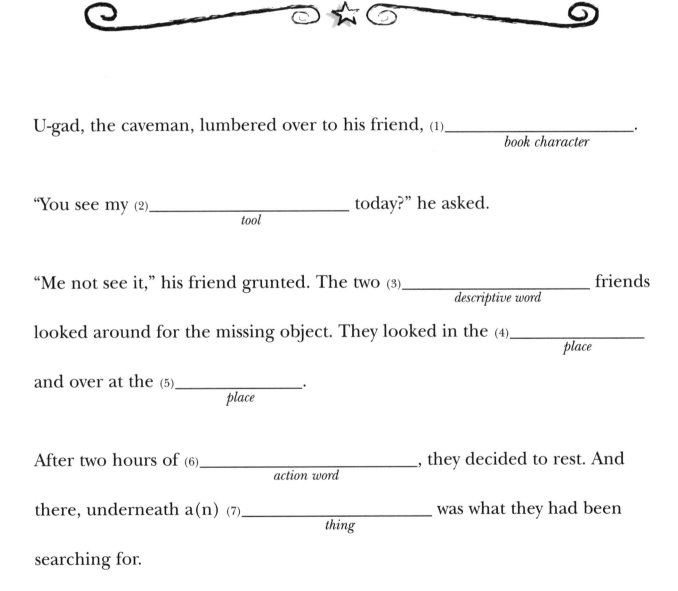

Anachronism Ad-libs

Class Activity — Part 2

Transfer the words from Part I to the blanks below. Read the newly created story. Are there any examples of anachronisms? Is the story humorous?

U-gad, the caveman, lumbered over to his friend, (1)_____.
book character

"You see my (2)_____ today?" he asked.
tool

"Me not see it," his friend grunted. The two (3)_____ friends
descriptive word

looked around for the missing object. They looked in the (4)_____
place

and over at the (5)_____.
place

After two hours of (6)_____, they decided to rest. And
action word

there, underneath a(n) (7)_____ was what they had been
thing

searching for.

Anachronism Activities

Part I

List five book titles that deal with time travel. *(5 points per title.)*

1. _____
2. _____
3. _____
4. _____
5. _____

Part II

If you could be transported to England during the fifteenth century right now, how might you be different from the people you encounter? *(5 points for each thing listed that would make you stand out in the 1600s.)*

1. _____
2. _____
3. _____
4. _____
5. _____

Part III

On a separate piece of paper, create an Anachronism Ad-lib activity for another student. There should be at least five word blanks to fill in. *(You will receive 30 points for creating your own Anachronism Ad-lib and 15 points for completing another student's Anachronism Ad-lib.)*

Part IV

On a separate piece of paper, answer the following questions in complete sentences. *(You can receive up to 10 points for each answer.)*

1. Do you think time travel is possible? Why or why not?
2. Do you think time travel is a good idea? Why or why not?
3. If you could travel back in time, what historical period would you visit? Why?
4. What is your favorite book about time travel?
5. Why do you think people have always been so fascinated by the idea of traveling back in time or into the future?

The Wizards' Guide to Periodical Literature

"To Miss Granger, wishing you a speedy recovery, from your concerned teacher, Professor Gilderoy Lockhart, Order of Merlin, Third Class, Honorary Member of the Dark Force Defense League, and five time winner of Witch Weekly's Most-Charming-Smile Award."
From a Note to Hermione *Harry Potter and the Chamber of Secrets*

Harry Potter and the Chamber of Secrets

by J. K. Rowling

Story Synopsis

Harry Potter's first year at Hogwarts is over and he must spend a miserable summer with his awful aunt, uncle and cousin. His misery is interrupted by an uninvited magical house elf named Dobby, who brings Harry warnings of the dangerous year to come. Soon after this, three of the Weasley brothers arrive in a magical flying car and take Harry to their warm and inviting home for the remainder of the summer. When he finally starts the school year it is, as predicted, perilous to Harry and his friends. The heir of Slytherin has opened the Chamber of Secrets. Students, ghosts and pets are being attacked and petrified. Hagrid, the over-large groundskeeper, and Harry are both suspects. A magic diary, a loyal phoenix, the captured Ginny Weasley and the enigmatic Tom Riddle all play a role as the story climaxes with Harry once again confronting and defeating the evil Lord Voldemort.

Introduction

The massive library at Hogwarts is full of ancient texts and magic books. The Wizard World also has current periodicals that keep the magical community apprised of people and events of interest. The newspaper, *The Daily Prophet,* has a wide readership. The magazine, *Witch Weekly,* is apparently a combination of the Muggle World's *Time* and *People* magazines.

Our young heroes at Hogwarts often find themselves in a position where they need to answer questions concerning things that have happened in the past. Having the skills to do this research is often imperative to their health and welfare. Is there a Wizards' Guide to Periodical Literature? If not, there most certainly should be.

Time Required 40 minutes

Objectives

- The students will be introduced to *The Readers' Guide to Periodical Literature* and the purpose it serves in research.

- The students will explore the characteristics and organization of *The Readers' Guide to Periodical Literature.*

Materials

- visual from page 35

- activity from page 36 (Create a transparency as well as copies for each student or group.)

- multiple volumes of *The Readers' Guide to Periodical Literature*

- pens and pencils

Procedure

1. Prepare for the lesson by collecting back volumes of *The Readers' Guide to Periodical Literature,* making the transparencies and running off the appropriate number of activity sheets.

2. Inform the students that the lesson will be about a tool that is used in researching information using periodicals. Remind the students that periodicals are newspapers and magazines that are published on a regular schedule.

3. Display the visual. Read the introduction to the students. Quickly review the sample entries. Solicit answers to the five questions. The answers are: 1. Couriers and Pets; 2. See also—barn owls and snowy owls; 3. *Wizard Weekly;* 4. S Bones; 5. "Taking Sides on the Issue of Magic."

4. Show the students the volumes of *The Readers' Guide to Periodical Literature* and explain that they will be using these books in the lesson.

5. Display a transparency of the activity. Read the directions to the students. Inform the students of the number of questions that you require be answered. You may require the students to answer the questions in a bingo pattern of their choosing or to answer a specific number of questions. This will depend on the students' ability and the time allocated for the lesson.

6. Remember, the objective of the lesson is to have the students become familiar with the existence of *The Readers' Guide to Periodical Literature.* It is enough that they are aware of its uses and structure.

7. Pass out the activity and a volume of *The Readers' Guide to Periodical Literature* to each student or group.

8. Allow at least 15 minutes to work on the assignment.

Evaluation

The answers to each student's or group's activity sheet will vary, depending on the volume of *The Readers' Guide to Periodical Literature* that was used.

If time allows, papers and volumes can be exchanged to check the work completed.

Extension

The following questions may be used for discussion or as the topic for a writing assignment.

Many libraries and classrooms currently use computer databases to store information from articles published in magazines and newspapers. Do you think a computer database is easier to use than *The Readers' Guide to Periodical Literature?* What are the advantages and disadvantages of using the computer? What are the advantages and disadvantages of using *The Readers' Guide to Periodical Literature?*

The Wizards' Guide to Periodical Literature

If a Wizards' Guide to Periodical Literature actually existed it would likely resemble the Muggle index called *The Readers' Guide to Periodical Literature*. This is a research tool that arranges entries alphabetically by subject and author. Each entry supplies the title of the article, author of the article, title of the publication in which the article appears, volume number of the periodical, pages of the article and other information.

Directions: Use the entries from the imaginary Wizard's Guide to Periodical Literature to answer the questions below.

OWLS

Couriers

Are owls the only way of communication? R Skitter. *Wizard Weekly* v34 no 15 p 23–48 Jan 14 '03

Keeping our messengers healthy. R Hagrid. *Amazing Animals Monthly* v123 p 90–97 D '02

Training owls properly. D Thomas. il *Bird and Bat Care Quarterly* v40 p33–39 J-M '03

Pets

The best owls to own in the city. S Bones. il *Magical Pets* v21 p45–9 D '02

See also
barn owls
snowy owls

OXFORD, NORWOOD

Taking sides on the issue of magic [cover story]. *Philosophical Issues* vol8 p 3–12

---

1. What are the two subtopics listed under the main subject "OWLS"?

   _____

2. Where else can you find information concerning certain types of owls?

   _____

3. What is the name of the periodical in which Rita Skitter published her article?

   _____

4. Who is the author of "The Best Owls to Own in the City"?

   _____

5. What is the name of the article written by Norwood Oxford?

   _____

The Readers' Guide to Periodical Literature

The Readers' Guide to Periodical Literature is a set of books that are published semimonthly with collective issues published quarterly and annually. This research tool arranges entries alphabetically by subject and author. Each entry supplies the title of the article, author of the article, title of the publication in which the article appears, volume number of the periodical, pages of the article and other information. Information about the abbreviations used in entries may be found at the front of each volume.

Directions: Using a volume of *The Readers' Guide to Periodical Literature,* answer the questions below to create a pattern specified by your teacher.

In what kind of order are the entries in your *Readers' Guide to Periodical Literature* arranged?	How many periodicals beginning with the letter "M" are indexed in your volume?	Your *Readers' Guide to Periodical Literature* includes indexing from what dates?	How many pages are in your volume of *The Readers' Guide to Periodical Literature?*	Write a page on which an article from *Time* magazine is listed as a source.
Who is the publisher of *The Readers' Guide to Periodical Literature?*	What page contains titles of articles about birds?	List the name and page of an entry that contains a "SEE ALSO" reference.	What does the abbreviation "tr" stand for?	What color is the cover of your volume of *The Readers' Guide to Periodical Literature?*
What does the abbreviation "il" mean when used in an entry?	What does the abbreviation "jt auth" stand for?	**Free Space**	Write the name of an author in your volume whose last name starts with "R."	What is the last entry on page 61 of your *Readers' Guide to Periodical Literature?*
Write the number of the page on which an article published in December or August is listed.	What is listed first in an entry, the page number or year of publication?	List the title of an article about an animal.	On what page can an article about a U.S. president be found?	Is there an author listed in your volume that has your last name?
What is the volume number of your *Readers' Guide to Periodical Literature?*	Is the magazine *Discover* indexed in your *Readers' Guide to Periodical Literature?*	What does the abbreviation "por" stand for when used in an entry?	Is there an article in your *Readers' Guide to Periodical Literature* about hurricanes?	What is the first entry on page 53 of your *Readers' Guide to Periodical Literature?*

Researching Symbols

A Character's Coat of Arms

*"Once a king or queen in Narnia, always a king or queen in Narnia.
Bear it well, Sons of Adam! Bear it well, Daughters of Eve!"*
Aslan the Lion *The Lion, the Witch and the Wardrobe*

The Lion, the Witch and the Wardrobe

by C. S. Lewis

Story Synopsis

The story takes place in England during World War II. Four siblings, Peter, Susan, Edmund and Lucy, have been sent to the safety of the country-side. They are not at the country estate of Professor Digory Kirke long when they accidentally enter a wardrobe and encounter the entry-way into the magical land of Narnia. Here they discover that all the unique creatures living in Narnia are suffering under a spell from the evil White Witch. This cold and calculating villain has created a land were it is always winter, but never Christmas. They also meet the brave and wise lion, Aslan, who is working to defeat the White Witch and return Narnia to peace and prosperity. The children prove their bravery in the battle and become Kings and Queens of Narnia. Eventually they return to England through the wardrobe and discover that the professor believes their tale of magical adventures. He foreshadows that they will someday return to the land of Narnia.

Introduction

After the battle in which the White Witch is defeated, Peter, Susan, Edmund and Lucy remain in Narnia and reign there for many years. Narnia, a magical land, medieval in nature, would probably have had a type of heraldry system. As in Europe in the Middle Ages, this system would use signs and symbols to represent significant characteristics of the person displaying a shield or flag. What symbols would be important? Would the colors used have meaning? Would there be a motto involved? What might Lucy's coat of arms look like?

Time Required 40–45 minutes

Objectives

- The students will be introduced to the concept of the symbolic communication found in medieval heraldry.

- The students will create a Character Coat of Arms and a Motto for a literary character.

- The students will be encouraged to research symbols and their meanings in appropriate reference books.

Materials

- visuals from pages 39–41

- activity from page 42 (One copy for each student.)

- pens, colored pencils, markers and/or crayons

- research books dealing with heraldry, symbols, knighthood and the Middle Ages

- encyclopedias and dictionaries

Procedure

1. Introduce the lesson by asking the students if there are any other methods of communicating than talking and reading. (Possible answers include: *sign language, signs, symbols, colors and gestures.*) Explain to the students that they will be participating in an activity that deals with signs and symbols.

2. Explain that **heraldry** is a system of using symbols that dates back to the Middle Ages. This system was first used on the battlefield for purpose of identification. It quickly became a complicated system that had its own special rules and regulations.

3. Display the visual from page 39. Ask the students to think of one of their favorite fictional characters. Ask them if they know their character well enough to know the character's initials, favorite thing, a unique characteristic about him or her and the order of birth in the family.

4. Define "motto," telling the students that it means "a short phrase or sentence that applies to some specific person or thing, a slogan or saying."

5. Display the visual from page 40. Explain how each of the symbols displayed on the coat of arms tells something about Lucy Pevensie, a character in *The Lion, the Witch and the Wardrobe* by C. S. Lewis.

6. Display the visual from page 41. Review these items with the students, explaining that this list is a very small example of the symbols that exist. Inform them that they may even make up their own symbols as long as they can explain their meaning.

7. Pass out the activity. Tell the students that they are to create a shield and motto for a fictional literary character. (Television and movie characters only count if they are based on a book.)

8. Encourage the students to use appropriate reference tools to research signs and symbols that may be used in their creations.

9. Allow them 15–20 minutes to work. They may share their creations with the class when they are complete. **Note:** This is an excellent activity to do in collaboration with the classroom teacher. It works well with units concerning the Middle Ages, communication or literary characters.

Evaluation

The completed activity sheets make an appealing display. The name of the character could be placed under the displayed Coat of Arms. The name would be hidden, only to be revealed by curious students. This makes an interesting and interactive bulletin board.

Extension

Interested students may be interested in investigating their family's coat of arms or in creating a personalized one of their own. If this is the case encourage them to use available print material. You may wish to be careful concerning Internet searches dealing with family history, some of these sites require registration fees and can be expensive.

Character Coat of Arms

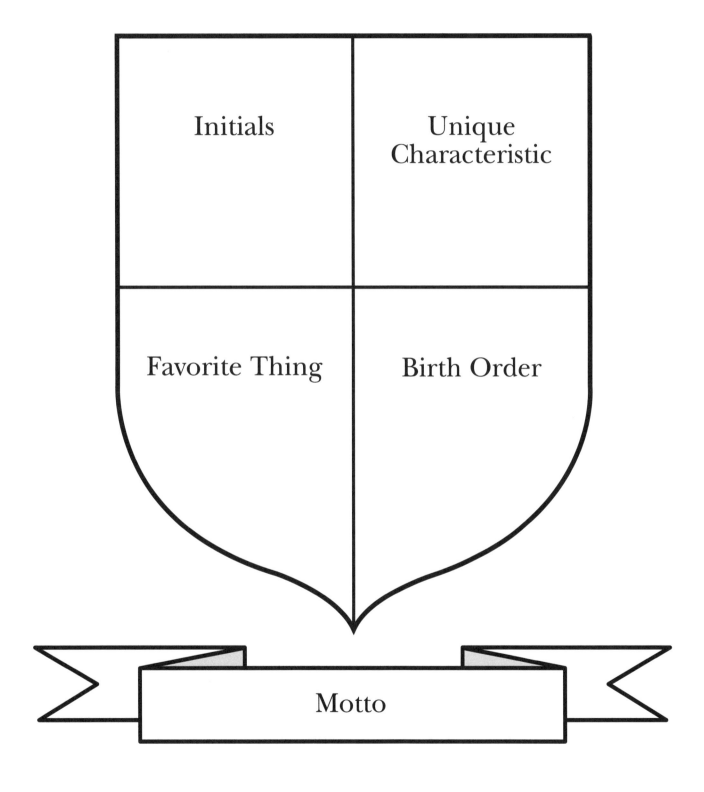

Initials

Unique
Characteristic

Favorite Thing

Birth Order

Motto

Character Coat of Arms

Lucy Pevensie's Narnian Coat of Arms

Queen Lucy the Valiant
~Friend to All~

Symbols & Interpretations

~· Animals ·~

- bear—strength
- bull—valor
- dragon—protection
- eagle—noble
- hawk—restless

- horse—prepared
- lion—dauntless courage
- ram—leader
- serpent—wise
- unicorn—bravery

~· Objects ·~

- arrow—readiness for battle
- castle—safety
- horseshoe—good luck
- lightning bolt—swiftness and power
- oak tree—strength

- rainbow—good following bad
- rock—protection
- sword—justice
- vine—strong friendship
- wheel—wealth

~· Colors ·~

- black—grief
- blue—loyalty
- gold—generosity
- green—hope and love
- orange—splendor

- purple—royalty
- red—bravery
- silver—peace
- white—purity and goodness
- yellow—betrayal

Character Coat of Arms

Create your own "Coat of Arms" for a favorite literary character using the example as a guide. Be prepared to explain your symbolism and motto.

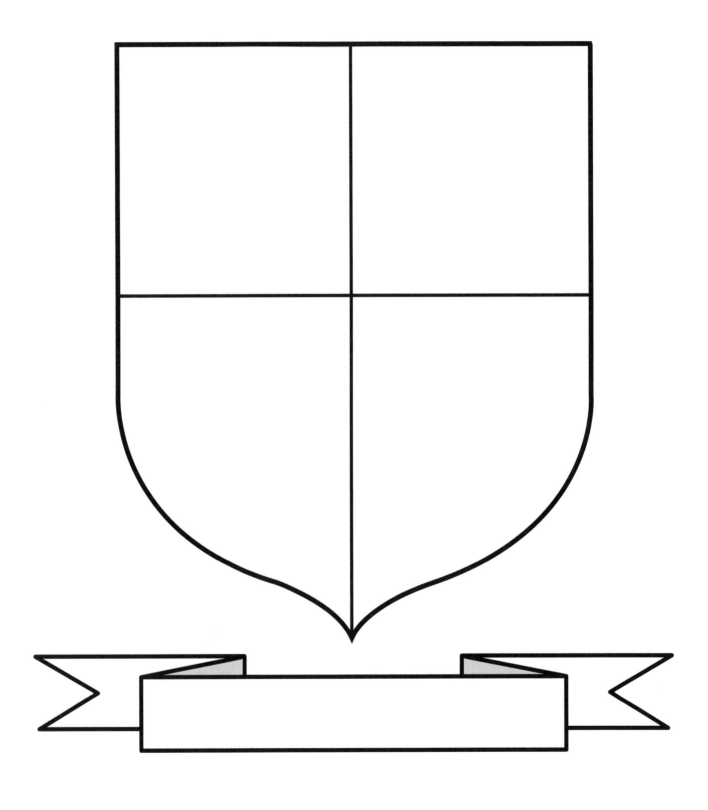

P.A.T.
Picking a Topic

"I say I noticed it—I did not pay any particular attention to it, for trucks were common enough in that part of town; but if I had, I would have noticed that printed on each side of it were four small letters: NIMH. I would not have known what they were, of course, for at that time neither I nor any of the other rats knew how to read."
Nicodemus the Rat *Mrs. Frisby and the Rats of NIMH*

Mrs. Frisby and the Rats of NIMH
by Robert C. O'Brien

Story Synopsis

Animals talk and rats **read** in this unusual Newbery Award winning book written by Robert C. O'Brien. *Mrs. Frisby and the Rats of NIMH* concerns a widowed field mouse, Mrs. Frisby, and her quest to relocate her family without jeopardizing the life of her young, sickly son, Timothy. To help her with this mission she consults the knowledgeable rats that live nearby. These literate animals, former subjects of scientific research and once residents of the laboratories at NIMH, develop a creative solution to her problem. In return, Mrs. Frisby is able to help them.

Introduction

The scientists in *Mrs. Frisby and the Rats of NIMH* were researchers by profession. The results from the experiments they conducted were recorded and evaluated for interpretation and use by others in the future. Students are researchers also. They are learning from others, thinking up ideas of their own and putting them together in distinctive ways. Before students take on a research project, it is a good idea for them to develop a topic that is realistic as well as interesting.

Time Required 35–45 minutes

Objectives

- The students will brainstorm a list of possible research topics.

- The students will evaluate and discuss the merit of listed topics.

Materials

- visuals from pages 46–48

- activity from page 49 (Enough copies for each student or group.)

- dice, cards or another device to be used for the random choice of a number between 1 and 6

- pencils or pens

- water-soluble marker

Procedure

1. Explain to the students that when they are assigned a research paper or project, they are often presented with a general subject and allowed to pick an aspect of the theme that appeals to them. This can be exciting but difficult. If the topic selected is too large, it will be difficult to narrow down. For example, the topic of "rats" is very broad. How could this topic be condensed to a three-page paper or a five-minute presentation? On the other hand, a very narrow topic such as "the food preference of rats living within a mile radius of the Empire State Building" would be difficult also. Where would you find this very specific information, if it existed at all?

2. Display the visual from page 46. Ask the students to volunteer suggestions for research topics dealing with the topic of "books." (Topic suggestions usually start out very broad, such as "the history of books" and then become more specific, "the parts of a book.") Record at least 10 suggestions on the transparency.

3. Display the visual from page 47. Discuss the similarities between the two lists. Use either or both lists, depending on the amount of time allocated for the lesson, to select five or more topics that would be interesting, but also relatively easy to research. The selections will vary from class to class, depending on topic selections and knowledge of materials available.

4. Pass out the activity and the dice. Students may work independently or in groups.

5. Display the visual from page 48. This is the stimulus for the activity.

6. Explain to the students they are to follow the directions at the top of the activity. Give the students 10 minutes to complete the activity.

7. Ask the students to share some of their more creative research topics with the class. For example, a student who rolled or picked block 5, George Washington, might suggest "Materials Used in Making False Teeth."

Evaluation

The students may share their topic suggestions with another student or with the group, depending on the remaining time.

If this lesson is an introduction to a research project that will be expanded on in the classroom, a master list of possible topics could be created at the conclusion of the lesson. Each student or group could record their favorite choices on index cards or a computer database.

Note: If working with a teacher on a specific area of study, it may be necessary to create another, more appropriate, six-block pictorial grid.

Extension

An acronym is a word formed from the first letters of other words, often used to name products or organizations. For example, the NIMH in *Mrs. Frisby and the Rats of NIMH* refers to the National Institute of Mental Health. Challenge the students to generate a list of as many acronyms as they can. Give them extra credit if they can find one for each letter of the alphabet.

Note: Most abbreviations are followed by a period. Until recently an acronym was one of the few exceptions. The popularity of IM or "instant messaging" has created a developing written language unique in computer communication. For example LOL is short for "Laughing Out Loud," YAC means "You Available to Chat?" and GABI stands for "Grin and Bear It." While these may not be on a current reference list of acknowledged acronyms, they may be in the near future. For this reason (and because it is interesting to be aware of the language of our youth) it is a good idea not to discount this new type of shorthand.

The following Web sites are good resources for this extension activity.

- www.acronymfinder.com
- www.ucc.ie/acronyms/
- www.acronymsearch.com

Sample Acronym List

- ASAP—As Soon As Possible
- BYTE—Binary Element String
- CURE—Citizens United for Racial Equality
- DVD—Digital Video Disc
- EPIC—Electronic Picture(s)
- FAT—Final Acceptance Test
- GOP—Grand Old Party (U.S. Republican Party)
- HIP—Health Insurance Plan
- IMP—Individual Meal Package
- JAG—Judge Advocate General
- KIP—Key Influence People
- LAF—Lost and Found
- MOP—Means of Production
- NASA—National Aeronautics and Space Administration
- OSHA—Occupational Safety & Health Administration
- POP—Point of Pressure
- QAR—Quick Access Recorder
- RIP—Rest In Peace
- SETI—Search for Extraterrestrial Intelligence
- TBA—To Be Announced
- UFO—Unidentified Flying Object
- VIP—Very Important Person
- WWW—World Wide Web
- XPAK—Expansion Pack
- YUPPIE—Young Urban Professional
- ZIP (Code)—Zone Improvement Plan

P.A.T.
Picking a Topic

Create a class list of possible research topics using the broad theme of "books."

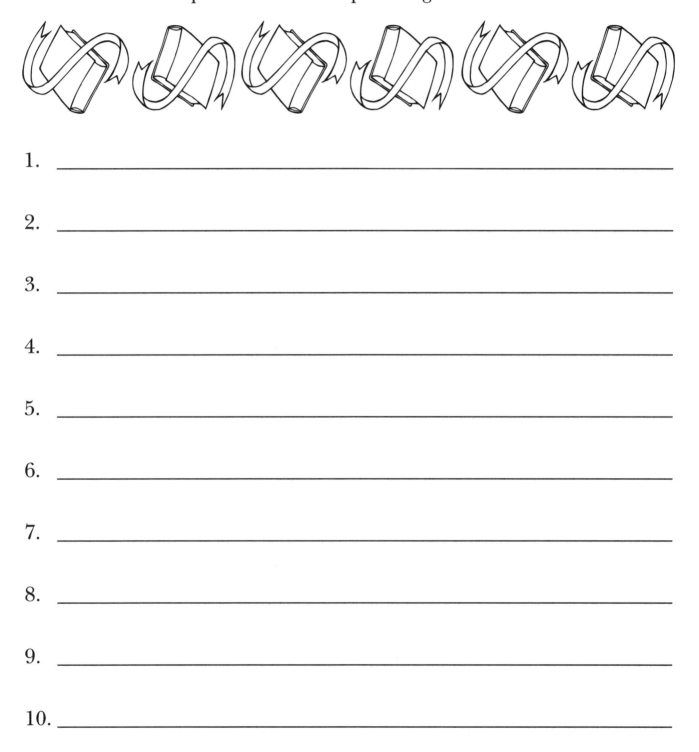

1. _____

2. _____

3. _____

4. _____

5. _____

6. _____

7. _____

8. _____

9. _____

10. _____

P.A.T.
Picking a Topic

Does your list look similar to the one below? Which topics do you think would be the easiest and most interesting to research? Why? Would any of the topics on either list be difficult to use? Why?

Illustrating Books

The Best Mystery Book of All Time

The History of Books

The Book Printing Process

Books in the Future

Book Publishing

How to Write a Book

The World's Largest Book

The World's Largest Library

Book Banning

The Most Popular Book

How to Make Paper

How to Design a Book Cover

This Year's Award Winning Books

What is a Book?

P.A.T.
Picking a Topic
Group Brainstorming Activity

P.A.T.
Picking a Topic
Group Brainstorming Activity

Pick a number between 1 and 6. Match your number to the box on the visual displayed. Brainstorm at least 15 topics that could be researched using the illustration in the box. Circle the five that you consider to be the best due to scope, interest and availability of information. Be prepared to share your results with the class.

1. _____

2. _____

3. _____

4. _____

5. _____

6. _____

7. _____

8. _____

9. _____

10. _____

11. _____

12. _____

13. _____

14. _____

15. _____

An Auspicious Autobiography

*"The book you are holding in your hands is extremely dangerous.
If the wrong people see you with this objectionable autobiography,
the results could be disastrous."*

Lemony Snicket *Lemony Snicket: The Unauthorized Autobiography*

Lemony Snicket: The Unauthorized Autobiography

by Lemony Snicket

Story Synopsis

Lemony Snicket: The Unauthorized Autobiography begins with a letter concerning the inaccurate report of the author's death in an unreliable newspaper, *The Daily Punctilio*. The rest of the 13-chapter book is full of many questions and the "primary sources" used to answer them. Incorporated in this tale are songs, photographs, letters, newspaper articles, maps and transcripts from secret meetings. Also included in this tongue-in-cheek book are a reversible book jacket, an unusual introduction and an interesting index. This book makes references to the characters in Snicket's Series of Unfortunate Events books and will be appreciated by those who are acquainted with the Baudelaire siblings.

Introduction

A biography is an account of a person's life as told by someone else whereas an autobiography is the story of a person's life as recounted by that person. *Lemony Snicket: The Unauthorized Autobiography* is written as if it were nonfiction, dealing with the mysterious life of the author. Because Lemony Snicket is actually the creation of Daniel Handler, the information in the autobiography is obviously fabricated (false and made-up). Nevertheless, it is an interesting puzzle. Will we ever find out the truth about the mysterious Mr. Lemony Snicket?

Time Required 30 minutes

Objectives

- The students will define biography and autobiography.

- The students will participate in a personal defining activity.

- The students will be encouraged to read age-appropriate biographies and autobiographies.

Materials

- visual from page 52

- activity from page 53

- pencils

- selection of biographies and autobiographies

- water-soluble marker

Procedure

1. Display the visual. Explain that a biography is an account of a person's life as told by someone else whereas an autobiography is the story of a person's life as recounted by that person. Inform the students that biographies and autobiographies are valuable tools when researching the life of a noted person.

2. Point out the list of shorter types of autobiographical writing (journals, diaries, logs, records, letters of correspondence, memoirs and chronicles).

3. Ask the students why a person might write an autobiography. Record their suggestions. (Possible answers: *They want to tell their side of the story. They want the money from writing a best-selling book. They wish to share their interesting life with others. They are conceited and are just showing off.*)

4. Indicate where the biographies are shelved in the library and show the students the selection of biographies and autobiographies that have been pulled from the collection. (You may allow the students to check these books out when they complete the activity.)

5. Pass out the activity. Read the introduction to the class. Allow 10 minutes for the completion of the activity. Students may work individually or in groups.

Evaluation

Students know that they may be called on to share their character with the class. (This keeps them from getting too outrageous.) Therefore, if time allows, ask for volunteers to read the "auspicious" character they have created. Ask the class if, indeed, this might be a person who would be able to write an autobiography worth reading.

Extension

The humorous title, *Lemony Snicket: The Unauthorized Autobiography,* is a contradiction. How can information written about a person, by that person, be unauthorized? In fact, the title is an example of an **oxymoron.** This is a figure of speech in which contradictory words are placed together for a curious effect. Examples include: virtual reality, even odds, original copy and first annual. Students who like to play with words can be challenged to do so with the worksheet on page 54. Have interested students complete the activity.

Note: There are several good Web sites that students may use for their research.

- www.oxymoronlist.com
- www.oxymorons.com.

An Auspicious Autobiography

A **biography** is an account of a person's life as told by someone else whereas an **autobiography** is the story of a person's life as recounted by that person.

⁓ Shorter types of autobiographical writing include: ⁓

journals and diaries

logs and records

letters of correspondence

memoirs and chronicles

⁓ Why might a person write an autobiography? ⁓

An Auspicious Autobiography

Lemony Snicket: The Unauthorized Autobiography is an account of the life of a fictional character created by the author. Create your own auspicious (favorable and complimentary) character for an autobiography (life story). Be prepared to share your creation with the class.

* Name: _____

* Date and Place of Birth: _____

* Family: _____

* Occupation: _____

* Claim to Fame: _____

* Do you think the person you created would be able to write an interesting autobiography? Why or why not?

_____

_____

_____

_____

_____

Jumbo Shrimp and Hot Chili at the Oxymoron Café

An eating establishment, the Oxymoron Café, is well known for its strange customers and weird menu. For example, a "pretty ugly" person wearing "tight slacks" might order "hot chili."

An **oxymoron** is a figure of speech in which contradictory words are placed together for an unusual effect. Create at least three people who might visit the Oxymoron Café. Who are they? What do they look like? Where do they work? What do they order? Include at least three oxymorons with each description.

1. _____
_____
_____
_____
_____

2. _____
_____
_____
_____
_____

3. _____
_____
_____
_____

The Marvelous Matilda

Fact and Opinion

"By the time she was three, Matilda had taught herself to read by studying newspapers and magazines that lay around the house. At the age of four, she could read fast and well and she naturally began hankering after books."
Matilda

Matilda
by Roald Dahl

Story Synopsis

Matilda Wormwood is a child prodigy, teaching herself to read by the time she is three. Her indifferent and neglectful parents have no idea that their young daughter is so brilliant when they enroll her in Crunchem Hall Primary School. It is here Matilda applies her untapped mental powers to rid the school of the malevolent headmistress, Miss Trunchbull. In the process she sees to it that her beloved teacher, Miss Honey, is restored to financial security.

Introduction

Matilda Wormwood may have been reading by the age of three, but even she admits she does not understand all that she reads. Does Matilda know that an opinion is a viewpoint or belief held by a person? Does she realize that facts can be checked out or verified to be true? This lesson will give the students the opportunity to do some research in the library as they look for facts to support an opinion.

Time Required 30 minutes

Objectives

- The students will be able to define and identify a statement of fact and a statement of opinion.

- The students will be able to create statements of fact and opinion based on a recently read piece of literature.

Materials

- visual from page 57

- activity from page 58 (A copy for each student or group.)

- pencils and/or pens

Procedure

1. Ask the students if they are familiar with *Matilda* by Roald Dahl. (Most will have read the book and/or seen the movie.) Explain that it is the story of a very bright young girl whose family does not appreciate her intellect.

2. Display the visual. Read and discuss it with the class.

3. Pass out the activity. Students may work individually or in groups.

4. Read the directions to the class. Ask if there are any questions. Allow the students 10 minutes to work.

5. Check the answers as a group.

Evaluation

Suggested answers for the activity:

Part I: 1 = F, 2 = F, 3 = O, 4 = F, 5 = O, 6 = F, 7 = O, 8 = F, 9 = O, 10 = F

Part II: Answers will vary.

Extension

Matilda read many books before she even started school. Mrs. Phelps, a friendly librarian, suggested titles for the books that Matilda read. Post the following list of some of the titles for the students to view. (A more extensive list may be found in "The Reader of Books," the first chapter of *Matilda*.)

Challenge the students to research and record 10 statements of fact concerning either the book or the author of one of these titles. They may use encyclopedias to conduct their research. After the facts have been researched and written, the students may develop several statements of opinion based on these facts.

1. *Oliver Twist* by Charles Dickens

2. *Jane Eyre* by Charlotte Bronte

3. *Pride and Prejudice* by Jane Austen

4. *Tess of the D'Ubervilles* by Thomas Hardy

5. *Kim* by Rudyard Kipling

6. *The Invisible Man* by H. G. Wells

7. *The Old Man and the Sea* by Ernest Hemingway

8. *The Sound and the Fury* by William Faulkner

9. *The Grapes of Wrath* by John Steinbeck

10. *Animal Farm* by George Orwell

The Marvelous Matilda
Fact and Opinion

Opinion: A statement that tells a person's viewpoint or belief. It cannot be proven true or false, but it can be supported by facts.

Fact: Anything that can be checked or verified to be true. A factual statement can be proven true with research by using books, the Internet, interviews and observation.

An example of an opinion:

> Matilda Wormwood was a very smart girl.

Facts supporting this opinion:

- She taught herself to read when she was three years old.

- She could mentally add and subtract four-digit numbers before entering school.

- She could multiply large numbers in her head by the age of five.

- She had a large vocabulary. (Example: In first grade she knew that "epicure" means "someone who is dainty with his eating.")

- It was possible for her to formulate limericks quickly and creatively.

The Marvelous Matilda
Fact or Opinion

Part I

Write "F" in the blank if the sentence is a statement of fact. Write "O" if it is stating an opinion.

_____ 1. Miss Trunchbull was in charge of Crunchem Hall Primary School.

_____ 2. Matilda could read by the age of three.

_____ 3. Businessmen are more important than educators.

_____ 4. Some birds can talk.

_____ 5. Librarians are kind, intelligent and well read.

_____ 6. Roald Dahl is a well-known author of children's literature.

_____ 7. *Matilda* is a better book than *James and the Giant Peach*.

_____ 8. A horse's heart beats 40 times a minute.

_____ 9. Spain has a better climate than England.

_____ 10. It is possible to turn back a car's odometer, making it appear newer.

Part II

Write two factual statements about a book you have recently read.

1. _____

   _____

2. _____

   _____

Write two statements of opinion about a book you have recently read.

1. _____

   _____

2. _____

   _____

Heroes and Villains in Jeopardy

"Remember Cedric. Remember, if the time should come when you have to make a choice between what is right and what is easy, remember what happened to a boy who was good, and kind, and brave, because he strayed across the path of Lord Voldemort. Remember Cedric Diggory."

Albus Dumbledore, Headmaster of Hogwarts
Harry Potter and the Goblet of Fire

Harry Potter and the Goblet of Fire

by J. K. Rowling

Story Synopsis

The story begins with a murder in a small village that has a strange effect on Harry Potter and his lightning bolt scar. Soon after this unnerving incident, Harry and Hermione accompany the Weasley family to the wizard world's sporting event of the year, the Quidditch World Cup. The bizarre events at this affair are climaxed by evidence that Lord Voldemort's minions have regrouped and are up to their old cruel tricks. After the unsettling events at the Quidditch World Cup, the young people return to Hogwarts. They start the school year off with the news that the historical Triwizard Tournament has been reinstated. Three wizard schools will be competing, each with a champion chosen by the magical Goblet of Fire. Surprisingly a fourth champion is named, Harry Potter. Throughout the year all four students compete in three dangerous tasks, which include fighting dragons, rescuing friends held hostage underwater and maneuvering through a magical maze. The last task, more dangerous than anyone anticipated, involves a showdown with the ever-stronger Lord Voldemort and the death of Hogwarts' other champion, Cedric Diggory.

Introduction

Interesting characters are the essence of any good story. It is the people, animals and even things that have human characteristics in a story that make it interesting. Most stories contain a hero or protagonist. This is the character that the reader identifies with and cheers on. Many stories also contain a villain or antagonist. This is the character who opposes the hero and the one who readers love to hate.

Time Required 40–45 minutes

Objectives

- The students will define the literary terms "protagonist" and "antagonist."

- The students will use previous knowledge of literary characters to participate in a class activity reinforcing the concept of hero and villain.

- The students may be exposed to new literary works.

Materials

- visual from page 61
- activity from pages 62–63
- water-soluble marker
- activity from page 64
- pencils

Procedure

1. Create a method for using the game cards from page 62 prior to the lesson. This may be done several ways. A transparency may be made using page 63 with sticky notes covering the answers in the categories. Or a game board can be created using 25 book pockets to file the answer cards in. (To facilitate easy replacement of the game cards, either write the category on the back of each card or run off each category on a different color of paper.)

2. Display the visual. Read the definitions to the students. Solicit the answers to the matching game at the bottom of the transparency. Using an overhead marker, connect the pairs. The answers are: Robin Hood—Sheriff of Nottingham; Jack—the Giant; Luke Skywalker—Darth Vader; Little Red Riding Hood—the Big Bad Wolf; Dorothy—Wicked Witch of the West.

3. Divide the class into three groups to play Hero and Villain Jeopardy. Each group will need a scorekeeper and a spokesperson. The spokesperson is responsible for conferring with the team members concerning the choice of game card and stating the question for the answer on the card. The questions will be book or story titles. For example: "What is Star Wars?" could be the question for the answer Darth Vader. If a team gives the incorrect book title, the next team gets the opportunity to ask the correct question and earn the points on the card. No points will be

deducted for incorrect answers. The scorekeepers keep a tally of the points earned for all three teams. Scores will be compared at the end. The team with the highest points wins.

4. The group with the oldest member may be team A. The group with the youngest member team B and the remaining group is team C.

5. Start with Team A. Read the answer on the card that is picked. (If it is not answered correctly, another team may volunteer the answer, with the possibility of receiving the points on the card. However, Team B will be the next one to choose from the game board, giving all teams equal opportunity to score.)

6. Continue play until time runs out and all game cards have been used.

Evaluation

Allow the three scorekeepers to compare their records. By having three students keeping score, a system of "checks and balances" is created.

If the scores are not consistent, encourage the teams to come to some sort of consensus. Using the final results from the scorekeepers, declare a class champion. The highest scoring team wins "bragging rights."

Extension

Heroes are often recognized and rewarded for their bravery and good deeds. On the other hand, villains are often punished or shunned for their wicked ways. After students read an interesting book containing strong characters, have them create an award for the hero and/or a wanted poster for the villain. (See the activity on page 65.) These may be displayed on a bulletin board for use as "teasers" to spur student interest in the book.

Literary Characters

Harry the Hero and Voldemort the Villain

The **protagonist** is the hero of the story. Harry Potter is the character that the reader "roots for" in J. K. Rowling's books.

The **antagonist** is the person or thing in conflict with the hero of the story. Lord Voldemort is the major villain or "destructive force" in the Harry Potter books.

Match the literary hero to the villain:

Hero—Protagonist	Villain—Antagonist

_____ Robin Hood   A. Darth Vader

_____ Jack   B. Wicked Witch of the West

_____ Luke Skywalker   C. Sheriff of Nottingham

_____ Little Red Riding Hood   D. The Giant

_____ Dorothy   E. The Big Bad Wolf

Hero and Villain Jeopardy
Game Cards

Wicked "Evil Doers"	Reluctant Heroes	Animal Villains	Fearless Females	Mean Monsters
10 Count Olaf	**10** Ron Weasley	**10** The Cheshire Cat	**10** Matilda Wormwood	**10** Fluffy the three-headed dog
20 Lord Voldemort	**20** Frodo Baggins	**20** Scabbers (also known as Wormtail)	**20** Dorothy from Kansas	**20** Smaug the Dragon
30 Captain Hook	**30** Mathias the Mouse	**30** Winged Monkeys	**30** Violet Baudelaire	**30** Headless Horseman
40 Jadis the White Witch	**40** Charlie Bucket	**40** Cluny the Scourge (a rat)	**40** Alice Liddell	**40** Cyclops
50 Professor Moriarty	**50** Will Parry	**50** Shelob the Spider	**50** Meg Murry (sister of Charles Wallace)	**50** Vampire

Hero and Villain Jeopardy
Questions

Wicked "Evil Doers"	Reluctant Heroes	Animal Villains	Fearless Females	Mean Monsters
10 What is … **A Series of Unfortunate Events** by Lemony Snicket?	**10** What is … the **Harry Potter** series by J. K. Rowling?	**10** What is … *Alice in Wonderland* by Lewis Carroll?	**10** What is … *Matilda* by Roald Dahl?	**10** What is … the **Harry Potter** series by J. K. Rowling?
20 What is … the **Harry Potter** series by J. K. Rowling?	**20** What is … **The Lord of the Rings** series by J. R. R. Tolkien?	**20** What is … the **Harry Potter** series by J. K. Rowling?	**20** What is … *The Wonderful Wizard of Oz* by L. Frank Baum?	**20** What is … *The Hobbit* by J. R. R. Tolkien?
30 What is … *Peter Pan* by J. M. Barrie?	**30** What is … *Redwall* by Brian Jacques?	**30** What is … *The Wonderful Wizard of Oz* by L. Frank Baum?	**30** What is … **A Series of Unfortunate Events** by Lemony Snicket?	**30** What is … *The Legend of Sleepy Hollow* by Washington Irving?
40 What is … *The Lion, the Witch and the Wardrobe* by C. S. Lewis?	**40** What is … *Charlie and the Chocolate Factory* by Roald Dahl?	**40** What is … *Redwall* by Brian Jacques?	**40** What is … *Alice in Wonderland* by Lewis Carroll?	**40** What is … *The Odyssey* by Homer?
50 What is … *The Adventures of Sherlock Holmes* by Sir Arthur Conan Doyle?	**50** What is … **His Dark Materials** series by Philip Pullman?	**50** What is … *The Lord of the Rings: The Two Towers* by J. R. R. Tolkien?	**50** What is … *A Wrinkle in Time* by Madeleine L'Engle?	**50** What is … *Dracula* by Bram Stoker?

Hero and Villain Jeopardy
Score Sheets

TEAM A	TEAM B	TEAM C
1. _____	1. _____	1. _____
2. _____	2. _____	2. _____
subtotal _____	subtotal _____	subtotal _____
3. _____	3. _____	3. _____
subtotal _____	subtotal _____	subtotal _____
4. _____	4. _____	4. _____
subtotal _____	subtotal _____	subtotal _____
5. _____	5. _____	5. _____
subtotal _____	subtotal _____	subtotal _____
6. _____	6. _____	6. _____
subtotal _____	subtotal _____	subtotal _____
7. _____	7. _____	7. _____
subtotal _____	subtotal _____	subtotal _____
8. _____	8. _____	8. _____
subtotal _____	subtotal _____	subtotal _____
9. _____	9. _____	9. _____
subtotal _____	subtotal _____	subtotal _____
10. _____	10. _____	10. _____
subtotal _____	subtotal _____	subtotal _____
11. _____	11. _____	11. _____
subtotal _____	subtotal _____	subtotal _____
12. _____	12. _____	12. _____
subtotal _____	subtotal _____	subtotal _____
13. _____	13. _____	13. _____
subtotal _____	subtotal _____	subtotal _____
14. _____	14. _____	14. _____
subtotal _____	subtotal _____	subtotal _____
15. _____	15. _____	15. _____
subtotal _____	subtotal _____	subtotal _____
TOTAL PTS. _____	TOTAL PTS. _____	TOTAL PTS. _____

Enrichment Activity
Harry the Hero and
Voldemort the Villain

Create a document for a fictional character that proves this person's good deeds or evil ways. This may be in the form of an award, a wanted poster, a newspaper article, etc. The document may be handwritten or computer generated. It must contain at least three facts concerning the character. Some examples are provided below.

WANTED

Voldemort
Lord of Darkness and Evil
a.k.a. Tom Riddle

LARGE REWARD

Last seen in the company of
Peter Pettigrew (a.k.a. Wormtail)

Note: Though he has no arms, in fact he has no body, he is still considered armed and dangerous.

**Awarded
to
Harry Potter**

A member of Gryffindor House.

In honor of winning the
Triwizard Tournament
and defeating Voldemort.

First Place

* Donated winnings to
Fred and George Weasley.

A Series of Clues

"You are learning something every day. A baby has brains, but doesn't know much. Experience is the only thing that brings knowledge, and the longer you are on earth the more experience you are sure to get.
The Wizard *The Wonderful Wizard of Oz*

The Wonderful Wizard of Oz

by L. Frank Baum

Story Synopsis

A cyclone transports young Dorothy and her dog, Toto, to the magical land of Oz. Alone and confused she soon befriends a Scarecrow, a Tin Woodman and a Cowardly Lion. The four join forces in their quest to find the Great Wizard of Oz, hoping he can help them with their individual problems—the Scarecrow wants a brain, the Tin Woodman thinks he needs a heart and the Lion would like some courage. Dorothy feels she must seek out the great wizard in order to return to Kansas. The wizard turns out to be a "humbug," but this does not keep the characters from realizing their wishes.

Introduction

Throughout *The Wonderful Wizard of Oz,* there are clues that let the reader come to the conclusion that the Scarecrow is actually very clever, the Tin Woodman extremely sentimental and the Cowardly Lion truly brave. This lesson is also full of clues. It can serve as a review of fantasy literature, a method of creating interest in reading or just a fun competitive activity. **Note:** The books in this lesson are mainstream and most students will recognize the titles.

Time Required 25–30 minutes

Objectives

- The students will participate in a competitive literature game.

- The students will review the literary terms of character, setting and theme.

- The students will discuss the characteristics of books written as a series.

Materials

- visuals from pages 68–71

- activity from page 72

- pencils or pens

- *optional*—copies of the books noted in the lesson available for students to check out

Procedure

1. Ask the students if they know what the characteristics of books written as a series are. (Possible answers: *The books are often written by the same author. The stories have the same characters. The plot continues from one book to the next.*) Try to keep them from giving specific titles.

2. Ask the students why they think books written in a series are so popular. (Possible answers: *Readers enjoy the author's style. Readers identify with the characters in the story. The story is so interesting that the reader wants to know more.*) Again, try to keep the students from giving specific titles.

3. Explain that this lesson will test their knowledge of books written in a series.

4. Display the visual from page 68, covering up all but the first clue (number five). Ask the students not to call out their answers. Read the first clue to the class. Ask for a show of hands of the students who may know the book title. Reveal the second clue (number four). Again ask the students if they have any ideas. Ask if anyone has changed his or her first guess. Continue with this process until all the clues have been read. Reveal the answer, *The Wonderful Wizard of Oz.*

5. Pass out the activity from page 72 to each student or group.

6. Explain to the students that you will display and read clues for eight books. (Visuals from pages 69–71.) They may write **one** guess on each line after each clue is given. They may change their answer on the next clue, but are not allowed to go back and change an answer to a previous clue. When all five clues have been given and the answer is revealed, they may circle the number next to the first time they wrote the correct title. **Note:** Give credit for "close enough" answers. For example, if a student writes A Series of Unlucky Events for # 2, give him or her credit.

Evaluation

The students can tabulate their scores by adding the eight circled numbers together and recording the total on their answer sheet.

Rating:

30–40—Excellent, True "Clue Master"

20–29—Very Good, Well-Read, Good Guesser

10–19—Fair, Passable Paper

0–9—Needs Improvement, Needs to Read More

Extension

Students may want to create clue lists of their own. The activity found on page 73 can be done in cooperative learning groups or used as part of a student interest center.

A Series of Clues

Can you name the book using the clues given?

5. The first book in the series was written over 100 years ago.

4. The story starts with a natural disaster.

3. Of the four main characters only one is human.

2. The theme of the book is "there's no place like home."

1. The author is L. Frank Baum.

~ Answer ~

> *The Wonderful Wizard of Oz*
>
> Other titles include: *The Marvelous Land of Oz* and *Ozma of Oz.*

- After what statement did you know the correct answer?

- The number in front of that statement is the number of points you would receive for this series of clues.

A Series of Clues

Clue Set 1

5. It is written as a series.

4. The books were not written in the order in which they happened.

3. The setting is the Isle of Terramort.

2. Many of the main characters are talking rodents.

1. The author is Brian Jacques.

Answer: The Adventures of Redwall Abbey series. Titles include: *Redwall, Marlfox, Martin the Warrior, The Legend of Luke* and *Mossflower.*

Clue Set 2

5. It is unhappily written as a series.

4. The main characters are orphans.

3. The main characters have many terrible adventures, but never age.

2. The villain in the stories is Count Olaf.

1. The author is Lemony Snicket, a.k.a. Daniel Handler.

Answer: A Series of Unfortunate Events. Some titles include: *The Bad Beginning, The Wide Window* and *The Miserable Mill.*

Clue Set 3

5. Seven books are planned for this series.

4. The primary setting is a private boarding school.

3. The main character is an orphan.

2. The theme is "good overcomes evil."

1. The author is J. K. Rowling.

Answer: The Harry Potter series. Some titles include: *Harry Potter and the Sorcerer's Stone, Harry Potter and the Goblet of Fire* and *Harry Potter and the Order of the Phoenix.*

A Series of Clues

Clue Set 4

5. There are two books in this "sweet" series.

4. The main characters are a poor boy and an eccentric entrepreneur.

3. The setting of the story is an industrial town in England.

2. The theme of the story is "goodness shall be rewarded."

1. The author is Roald Dahl.

Answer: *Charlie and the Chocolate Factory* and/or *Charlie and the Glass Elevator.*

Clue Set 5

5. This series was written as a trilogy.

4. Characters include wizards, elves, trolls and dwarfs.

3. The story takes place in the Third Age of Middle-earth.

2. The author created a special alphabet and language as part of the story.

1. The author is J. R. R. Tolkien.

Answer: The Lord of the Rings Trilogy. Titles include: *The Fellowship of the Ring, The Two Towers* and *The Return of the King.*

Clue Set 6

5. This "dark" series includes three books.

4. Using special tools, main characters are able to travel into other worlds.

3. A theme is "sacrifices must be made for the greater good."

2. Characters include witches, angels and armored bears.

1. The author is Phillip Pullman.

Answer: His Dark Materials series. Titles include: *The Golden Compass, The Subtle Knife* and *The Amber Spyglass.*

A Series of Clues

Clue Set 7

5. The book is the first of many about this family of gifted scientists.

4. Characters include a small boy, the evil IT and extraterrestrial "witches."

3. The book starts with the sentence, "It was a dark and stormy night."

2. The story includes the theory of space travel using the tesseract.

1. The author is Madeleine L'Engle.

Answer: *A Wrinkle in Time*. Other titles in the Time Quartet include: *A Wind in the Door*, *A Swiftly Tilting Planet* and *Many Waters*.

Clue Set 8

5. The series involves the adventures of four English schoolchildren.

4. The hero is a magnificent golden lion.

3. The evil white witch makes sure it is always winter but never Christmas.

2. The entryway to a magical realm is through a wardrobe.

1. The author is C. S. Lewis.

Answer: The Chronicles of Narnia. Titles include: *The Magician's Nephew; The Lion, the Witch and the Wardrobe; The Horse and His Boy; Prince Caspian; The Voyage of the Dawn Treader; The Silver Chair* and *The Last Battle*.

A Series of Clues
Answer Sheet

Clue Set 1

5. _____

4. _____

3. _____

2. _____

1. _____

Clue Set 2

5. _____

4. _____

3. _____

2. _____

1. _____

Clue Set 3

5. _____

4. _____

3. _____

2. _____

1. _____

Clue Set 4

5. _____

4. _____

3. _____

2. _____

1. _____

Clue Set 5

5. _____

4. _____

3. _____

2. _____

1. _____

Clue Set 6

5. _____

4. _____

3. _____

2. _____

1. _____

Clue Set 7

5. _____

4. _____

3. _____

2. _____

1. _____

Clue Set 8

5. _____

4. _____

3. _____

2. _____

1. _____

Create Your Own Author, Book or Character Clues

1. Choose one of the topics listed in the title above.

2. Pick a particular subject in the topic.

3. Think of five facts unique to that subject.

4. List them from most general to most specific.

5. Quiz others using your list.

6. Award points by using the number that corresponds to the clue number at which the correct answer was given.

Clues

5. _____

4. _____

3. _____

2. _____

1. _____

The Protagonist Problem

A Matter of Point of View and Perspective

"At the castle the king locks the girl into a room and tells her,
'Spin this straw into gold or tomorrow you die.'
Not my idea of a promising first date."
Vivian Vande Velde *The Rumpelstiltskin Problem*

The Rumpelstiltskin Problem

by Vivian Vande Velde

Story Synopsis

The author, Vivian Vande Velde, asks some very interesting questions in her Author's Note at the beginning of *The Rumpelstiltskin Problem*. She rightfully questions the entire premise of the traditional Rumpelstiltskin tale. Why would a caring father tell such an obvious untruth about his beloved daughter? If his daughter could spin straw into gold, how is it they were not wealthy? Why would Rumpelstiltskin accept the payment of a gold ring for his labor when he could spin gold anytime he chose to? Would a reasonable young woman marry someone who had threatened to cut off her head the day before? To make some sense of this illogical tale, the author has written six alternative adaptations, each featuring a distinctly different Rumpelstiltskin.

Introduction

A lunch tray crashes to the floor in a crowded school cafeteria. The story of what happens following this incident changes considerably when told from the perspective of the different people who witnessed the event. The new student who dropped the tray will tell a tale of embarrassment and social ruin. The class clown watching the new student's face turn bright red will be delighted because a cruel nickname has just formed in her mind and she can not wait to share it with all of the school's popular students. The school custodian views the whole incident as a bother, but is happy the student had a salad and sandwich instead of the spaghetti and grape juice.

The author of a story decides which character will be the protagonist, or hero, of the tale being told. Thus the same event could become a tragedy, joke or insignificant event, depending on whose voice we hear.

Time Required 35–40 minutes

Objectives

- The students will be able to define protagonist, antagonist, first person and third person point of view

- The students will create an alternate view to a well-known tale.

Materials

- visuals from pages 77–78

- activity from page 79 (Run off on card stock and cut prior to lesson.)

- paper and pencils

- *optional*—copies of the following tales for student reference:

  - The Adventures of Robin Hood and His Merry Men

  - Cinderella

  - Goldilocks and the Three Bears

  - Hansel and Gretel

  - The Frog Prince

  - Jack and the Beanstalk

  - Little Red Riding Hood

  - The Little Red Hen

  - Snow White and the Seven Dwarfs

  - The Three Little Pigs

  - The Ugly Duckling

Procedure

1. Introduce the lesson by asking the students if they have ever heard the fairy tale Rumpelstiltskin. (Most will have.) You may want to have a student give a brief synopsis of the story.

2. Tell the students that the lesson will be dealing with point of view and perspective and that some vocabulary will need to be learned before proceeding.

3. Display the visual from page 77. Read and discuss the definitions with the class.

4. Display the visual from page 78. Read and discuss it with the class. Ask the students if they can think of another character that might tell the story. A student may suggest that a narrator could tell the story. Explain that this would be an example of third person point of view.

5. Divide the students into groups and allow them to pick a card. This may be done randomly, or you may make a transparency of the activity and allow groups to choose the tale they would like to work with. **Note:** This lesson may be done by individual students, but more interactive learning takes place when groups work on and present their solutions.

6. Have the students use the tale described to write a story, create a poem or perform a skit that explains the situation from the point of view of the character on the card. They should be prepared to share their work with the class.

7. Allow the students 10–15 minutes of working time. (Each presentation usually takes 2–4 minutes.)

Evaluation

The following criteria may be used to score the solution.

Was it possible to identify …?

The Tale:

- Easily—10 points

- Somewhat—5 points

- Not at all—0 points

The Protagonist:

- Easily—10 points

- Somewhat—5 points

- Not at all—0 points

The Problem:

- Easily—10 points

- Somewhat—5 points

- Not at all—0 points

Bonus points: Total team participation is worth 10 extra points.

Extension

Have students create a newspaper that features fairy tales and folklore from the point of view of unexpected characters featured in these stories. For example, the giant in Jack in the Beanstalk may be portrayed as the victim of robbery and vandalism. Cinderella's stepmother could be concerned that her unappreciative charge ran away without permission and is asking the public for help in locating her. A story about poor senior citizens living alone, as the witch does in Hansel and Gretel, may describe the problem of young ruffians taking advantage of the elderly.

The Protagonist Problem
Perspective and Point of View

~· Protagonist ·~

The hero or main character of a story.

~· Antagonist ·~

A person or thing working against the protagonist, often referred to as the villain.

~· Problem ·~

A difficulty, dilemma or puzzle that needs to be solved.

~· Point of View ·~

The angle from which the story is told.

- **First person point of view** means that one of the characters is telling the story from their perspective, or through what they see or know. Words such as I, my and we are used in first-person narratives.

- **Third person point of view** means that the storyteller is viewing what is occurring and sharing this information. Words such as she, he and they are used to reveal what the characters are doing.

The Protagonist Problem
Perspective and Point of View

How a story is told often depends on who is telling the tale. For example:

> # Rumpelstiltskin

If the story is told in first person through the eyes of …

… **The miller's daughter**—then she is a survivor who cares for her firstborn child above all else.

… **Rumpelstiltskin**—then he may be someone who has been cheated out of payment for a job well done.

… **The king**—then he may be wondering what is upsetting his wife. She has not spun straw into gold in a very long time and is so nervous since the baby was born.

… **The miller**—then you may hear a tale about a father who is sorry he ever made all those untrue statements about his beloved daughter. However, now that she is married to the king, it may have been all for the best.

Protagonist and Problem Cards

Tale Goldilocks and the Three Bears **Protagonist** Baby Bear **Problem** You are starting to feel very picked on. Why is it always your porridge, your chair and your bed?	**Tale** Little Red Riding Hood **Protagonist** Red Riding Hood's Mother **Problem** You have a silly daughter who will not follow instructions, cannot tell the difference between her grandmother and a wolf and talks to strangers.	**Tale** The Little Red Hen **Protagonist** The Cat **Problem** What is wrong with that selfish chicken? Why won't she share that wonderful freshly baked bread?
Tale The Three Little Pigs **Protagonist** The Big Bad Wolf **Problem** You have new neighbors who are making too much noise and mess as they construct poorly built houses.	**Tale** Snow White and the Seven Dwarfs **Protagonist** The Queen **Problem** Your unfeeling stepdaughter enjoys making you feel old and look unattractive.	**Tale** Frog Prince **Protagonist** The Princess **Problem** No one could expect you to keep your promise to an ugly frog. You could get warts!
Tale The Adventures of Robin Hood and His Merry Men **Protagonist** The Sheriff of Nottingham **Problem** You keep getting robbed while traveling in the forest.	**Tale** The Ugly Duckling **Protagonist** Mother Duck **Problem** One of your babies is very awkward and unattractive. You feel miserable for him, but you are having a hard time liking him.	**Tale** Your Choice **Protagonist** Your Choice **Problem** Your Choice

Genre
Science Fiction and Fantasy

"For things that are seen are temporal,
but things that are unseen are eternal."
Aunt Beast *A Wrinkle in Time*

A Wrinkle in Time
by Madeleine L'Engle

Story Synopsis

A Wrinkle in Time by Madeleine L'Engle won the Newbery Award in 1963. This book is a very good example of one that can legitimately be classified into the categories of science fiction and fantasy. The story is the classical tale of good vs. evil. Our heroine, Meg Murry, a misfit at school, misses her scientist father, who has vanished "off the face of the earth." She learns her own strength of character as she, her youngest brother, Charles Wallace, and their new friend, Calvin, join forces with three extraterrestrials to save the world.

Introduction

Genre is a type of literary composition defined by its subject matter. Science fiction and fantasy are often grouped together into one genre classification. While both deal with stories that are astonishing and mind-boggling, they are very different. Science fiction stories may include characters, problems and settings that are all "out of this world" but they can all be explained scientifically. On the other hand, fantasy stories use unexplainable magic to solve problems and save the day.

Time Required 30 minutes

Objectives

- The students will be introduced to literary genre in general and the genres of science fiction and fantasy specifically.

- The students will be involved in an interactive activity that will reinforce the concept introduced.

Materials

- visuals from pages 82–83

- game cards from pages 84–85

- transparency marker or highlighter

Procedure

1. Prior to the lesson, photocopy the game cards from pages 84–85 and have them cut and ready for class. Be sure to keep a master copy of the cards for use in identifying the correct answers.

2. Display the visual from page 82. Read and discuss the information on it with the students.

3. Ask the students if they can recall ever having read science fiction and fantasy stories. Many will have seen movies that are in these genres. The Star Wars and Star Trek movies would be classified as science fiction. The Lord of the Ring and Harry Potter films are both in the fantasy genre.

4. Divide the students into two groups. Decide which half will be the X group and which half the O group.

5. Explain that the class is going to play a tic-tac-toe game using the information concerning science fiction and fantasy.

6. Display the visual from page 83. Explain the directions and rules to the class. (The grid on the sheet may be made into a transparency and used to play the game.)

7. The group with the oldest student in it will go first.

8. Draw a game card from the deck of cards and read it to the first group. The group must identify it correctly as an example of either fantasy or science fiction.

9. If they are correct, they may place an X or O on the grid. If they are incorrect, they forfeit their turn and it is the next group's turn. A new card is read and the second group has the opportunity to identify it as fantasy or science fiction.

10. Repeat the pattern until one group succeeds in getting three X's or O's in a row.

Evaluation

After the game is completed and a winning team has been established, there may be game cards remaining. Read these to the students to see if these cards can be identified correctly.

Extension

Encourage the students to create their own game cards to use in the class tic-tac-toe game.

Genre
Science Fiction and Fantasy

Genre is a type of literary composition defined by its subject matter. Types of genre include adventure, mystery, romance and war stories.

Science fiction and **fantasy** stories are sometimes grouped together in the same genre even though there are some obvious differences.

⸗· Science Fiction ·⸗

Plot: The events of the story are often set in the future. While many of the situations and objects in the story do not actually exist, they can be explained scientifically.

Place: It is possible that the setting may exist, either on this planet, in our solar system or in a galaxy far away.

People: The characters may not all be human, but they can be explained scientifically. For example: Robots and Androids.

Problem: The problems in the story are usually solved using factual information and scientific procedures.

⸗· Fantasy ·⸗

Plot: The events of the story are often fantastic, could never have logically happened and are explained by the existence of magic.

Place: The setting of the story is often in an imaginary place on Earth during an unspecified time in the past.

People: The characters include members of the magical world such as wizards, trolls, elves and giants.

Problem: The problems in the story are usually enchantingly solved by using magic.

Genre
Science Fiction and Fantasy

Tic-Tac-Toe Grid

Genre
Science Fiction and Fantasy

Science Fiction Clues

No one knew that the brilliant pilot of the airship was actually a very lifelike robot.	While on a field trip to Thomas Jefferson's home Monticello, three students discover a time machine in the cellar.	Strange, unpleasant and very large plants were starting to grow near the toxic waste dump outside of town.
He hated living on Mars. It was always so cold but he had not seen snow for over 10 years.	As soon as Victor knew that it was his clone that had broken into the ambassador's top-secret computer files, he understood why he was in so much trouble.	Now that all the fossil fuels had been depleted, energy from Earth's core was being used to power most of Earth's generators.
Machines now were operating almost all of the world's factories and most of the population was unemployed.	There had been no real food on Earth for many years. Humans received all their nourishment from super nutritious pills.	The earth's underwater cities were now more populated than the polluted cities on the land.

Genre
Science Fiction and Fantasy

Fantasy Clues

A wizard's wand and some weird words change a small mouse into a huge elephant.	If a special pixie dust is sprinkled on a person's head at midnight, that person will be able to fly until sunrise.	Lead can be changed into gold by using charms and a unique ancient recipe.
When a shy young boy touches a special coin, he is transported to a new world where he is smart, strong and brave.	It is possible to use an enchanted watch to travel into the past and into the future to change history.	A dragon living in a cave is guarding a treasure she has taken from giants, trolls, goblins and elves.
The old lamp that the poor boy bought at an auction is the home of a genie who is willing to grant him three wishes.	The hateful witch cast a spell on a handsome prince, turning him into an old ugly toad.	While the Smiths sleep, their dog, cat and lizard, talk about how to help with a family problem.

The Rodent Reader's Award

A joyous chattering broke out among the Animals, but stilled when the Man quietly rose and approached the tarpaulin. Very deliberately he loosed its fastenings and flung it clear. In the deep silence that followed it was almost possible to hear the sound of a hundred little breaths caught and released in a sigh of awe.
The unveiling of the Francis of Assisi statue *Rabbit Hill*

Rabbit Hill

by Robert Lawson

Story Synopsis

New folks are moving in and the animals living on Rabbit Hill are very excited. This 1945 Newbery Award winning book, written and beautifully illustrated by Robert Lawson, contains animals that talk to each other as they try to figure out how to interact with the family that moved into a house that has been empty too long.

Introduction

Students understand that we live in a competitive society that rewards talent and hard work. They are accustomed to seeing the things that entertain them such as movies, television programs and music, which receive accolades for creativity and uniqueness. A method of proving that a good book can be as much entertainment as a popular movie is to teach the students that literature has its own recognitions and awards.

Time Required 35–40 minutes

Objectives

- The students will learn about literary awards and the Newbery Award specifically.

- The students will create a fictitious literary award associated with actual book titles.

- The students will verbally rationalize the choice of an answer in true or false questions.

Materials

- visuals from pages 88–89

- activity from page 90

- pencils

- *optional*—copies of Newbery Award winning books for display and checkout

Procedure

1. Display the visual from page 88, and ask the students to quickly read the list of titles and authors of Newbery Award winning books.

2. Explain that the first Newbery Medal was presented in 1922. Every year since, one children's book has won this prestigious award given by the American Library Association. Have the students analyze the list to see if they can determine what types of books win this award. Ask the following True/False questions and have the students include the reasoning for their answer.

   True or False: Only male authors can win this award. *False. Both male and female names are included on the list. (If the students ask, Avi is a male author.)*

   True or False: It is possible to win this award more than one time. *True. Lois Lowry won in 1990 and 1994.*

   True or False: Only fiction stories are allowed to win. *False.* Lincoln: A Photobiography *by Russell Freedman is a nonfiction book and* Joyful Noise: Poems for Two Voices *is a book of poems.*

   True or False: Authors who are related to each other are ineligible for this award. *False. Sid and Paul Fleischman are father and son.*

   True or False: Only books written by American authors can receive a Newbery Award. *True. This is why books written by Roald Dahl, Brian Jacques, Philip Pullman and J. K. Rowling will never win a Newbery Award.*

3. Display the visual from page 89.

4. Read the visual to the students. Ask them what clues indicate that this is not a real literary award. (Possible answers: *It sounds silly. Is there really an association called Major International Cheese Entrepreneurs? Would an author want to win a lifetime supply of cheese?*)

5. Explain that while this literary award does not exist, the books that **could** have won the award do.

6. Tell the students that they are now going to create their own literary award and pass out the activity. It may be done individually or in groups.

7. Inform the students that their award may be as silly or as serious as they choose, but that they will be sharing their ideas with the class, therefore they need to be kind. Allow 15 minutes for this part of the activity. Students should be encouraged to consult the patron's catalog or bookshelves for information concerning authors and titles.

Evaluation

Students have fun sharing the newly created literary awards. Bonus points are given to worksheets that include authors and copyright titles with the book titles.

Extension

Inquisitive students may be curious about literary awards in general. They may wish to know more about the many award programs. A good Internet site to allow students to investigate is www.literature-awards.com. Here they will find the many literary awards defined, a listing of the award winning books and links to sites with more specific information.

Newbery Award Winning Books

1985–2004

2004 *The Tale of Desperaux: Being the Story of a Mouse, a Princess, Some Soup and a Spool of Thread* by Kate DiCamillo

2003 *Crispin: The Cross of Lead* by Avi

2002 *A Single Shard* by Linda Sue Park

2001 *A Year Down Yonder* by Richard Peck

2000 *Bud, Not Buddy* by Christopher Paul Curtis

1999 *Holes* by Louis Sachar

1998 *Out of the Dust* by Karen Hesse

1997 *The View From Saturday* by E. L. Konigsburg

1996 *The Midwife's Apprentice* by Karen Cushman

1995 *Walk Two Moons* by Sharon Creech

1994 *The Giver* by Lois Lowry

1993 *Missing May* by Cynthia Rylant

1992 *Shiloh* by Phyllis Reynolds Naylor

1991 *Maniac Magee* by Jerry Spinelli

1990 *Number the Stars* by Lois Lowry

1989 *Joyful Noise: Poems for Two Voices* by Paul Fleischman

1988 *Lincoln: A Photobiography* by Russell Freedman

1987 *The Whipping Boy* by Sid Fleischman

1986 *Sarah Plain and Tall* by Patricia MacLachlan

1985 *The Hero and the Crown* by Robin McKinley

The Rodent Reader's Award

✎ The Award ✎

The Rodent Reader's Award is funded by the Major International Cheese Entrepreneurs (MICE). The selection committee consists of 10 members of this organization and past winners of this award. The prize for this annual award is a lifetime supply of cheese.

✎ Award Criteria ✎

1. At least one of the book's main characters must be or must have been a rodent.

2. The author must have written the book in English.

3. The book must be a chapter book written for young people.

✎ Past Winners ✎

1945 *Stuart Little* by E. B. White

1965 *The Mouse and the Motorcycle* by Beverly Cleary

1970 *Runaway Ralph* by Beverly Cleary

1971 *Mrs. Frisby and the Rats of NIMH* by Robert C. O'Brien

1986 *Redwall* by Brian Jacques

2000 *I Was a Rat!* by Philip Pullman

2001 *Rat Boys: A Dating Experiment* by Thom Eberhardt

2003 *The Tale of Desperaux* by Kate DiCamillo

Announcing a New Literary Award!

_____

Award Name

⌐ The Award ⌐

Write a statement that answers the following three questions.
Who sponsors the award? Who are the judges? What is the prize?

1. _____

2. _____

3. _____

⌐ Award Criteria ⌐

List at least three conditions that the award-winning book must meet.

1. _____

2. _____

3. _____

⌐ Past Winners ⌐

List at least three actual books that may have won this literary award had it existed.
Authors and copyright dates are optional.

1. _____

2. _____

3. _____

Book List

Centaur Aisle by Piers Anthony. Ballantine Books, 1981.

Harry Potter and the Chamber of Secrets by J. K. Rowling. Scholastic, 1999.

Harry Potter and the Goblet of Fire by J. K. Rowling. Scholastic, 2000.

Harry Potter and the Sorcerer's Stone by J. K. Rowling. Scholastic, 1998.

Lemony Snicket: The Unauthorized Autobiography by Lemony Snicket. HarperCollins, 2002.

The Lion, the Witch and the Wardrobe by C. S. Lewis. HarperCollins, 1994.

Matilda by Roald Dahl. Viking, 1988.

Max and Me and the Time Machine by Gery Greer and Bob Ruddick. Harcourt, 1983.

Mrs. Frisby and the Rats of NIMH by Robert C. O'Brien. Simon & Schuster, 1976.

Mummies in the Morning by Mary Pope Osborne. Random House, 1993.

The Phantom Tollbooth by Norton Juster. Knopf, 1976.

Rabbit Hill by Robert Lawson. Puffin, 1977.

The Rumpelstiltskin Problem by Vivian Vande Velde. Scholastic, 2002.

The Wonderful Wizard of Oz by L. Frank Baum. HarperCollins, 2000.

A Wrinkle in Time by Madeleine L'Engle. Farrar, Straus and Giroux, 1976.